Tucson Hiking Guide

Tucson Hiking Guide

Betty Leavengood

PRUETT PUBLISHING COMPANY
BOULDER, COLORADO

For information about permission to reproduce selections from this book, write to Permissions, Pruett Publishing Company, 2928 Pearl Street, Boulder, CO 80301.

Library of Congress Cataloging-in-Publication Data

Leavengood, Betty, 1939-
      Tucson hiking guide / Betty Leavengood.
        p.   cm.
      Includes bibliographical references and index.
      ISBN 0-87108-810-x (pbk.)
        1. Hiking — Arizona — Tucson Region — Guide-books. 2. Hiking
—Arizona — Tucson Region — Safety measures. 3. Tucson Region —
Description and travel — Guide-books.   I. Title.
GV199.42.A72T835   1991
917.91'776 —dc20   91-13851
                                                       CIP

Printed in United States of America

10 9 8 7 6 5 4 3

Cover Design by Ann E. Green, Green Design, Boulder Colorado
Book Design by Jody Chapel, Cover to Cover Design, Denver, Colorado

All photographs courtesy of the author.

Contents

The Santa Rita Mountains:

Preface

The day I got lost two miles from a major street and within sight of Tucson was the day I started thinking about this hiking guide. Several years ago I took my son and a friend on a hike to Little Wild Horse Tank. "It is," I expounded, "one of the prettiest spots in the Rincons. It's only 3.9 miles from the end of Broadway, and we can be there and back before noon." I should have paid attention to the hesitancy in my friend's voice when she asked, "Are you sure you know how to get there?"—especially as I had forgotten my map, a fact I did not at that point divulge.

We met at 7:00 A.M. at the Cactus Forest trailhead near the end of Broadway Boulevard, struck out on the Pink Hill Trail, and within two miles were hopelessly wandering about in the foothills of the Rincon Mountains. "Let's head for that canyon over there," I suggested, and we did. Two hours later we had scrambled over three ridges (all covered with shindaggers), slid down into deep arroyos, climbed out on all fours, and were nowhere in sight of Little Wild Horse Tank!

An hour later I was hiking far ahead of my friend whose last words before we separated were, "I hate to bushwack." I had judiciously placed my six-foot two-inch, 180-pound son between us. Another hour into this supposed four-hour hike and I finally stumbled down into upper Wild Horse Canyon. An hour's steep bushwacking down the canyon and we were seated by beautiful Little Wild Horse Tank, only 3.9 miles and five hours from Broadway Boulevard! It would take us nearly two more hours to return.

I started out to write and present to my friend the definitive guide to Little Wild Horse Tank and ended up with this *Tucson Hiking Guide,* a selection of thirty-three hikes for the "Sunday hiker." And what is a Sunday hiker? Someone who enjoys getting into the out-of-doors but who is not too familiar with the terrain and needs specific directions . . . a hiker who doesn't feel real comfortable with a compass and a point in the right direction . . . a person who likes to smell the roses . . . and someone who, when passing an old mine or abandoned house, wants to know what was mined there and who lived in that house.

So I undertook to write the Sunday hiker's guide to hiking in the four mountain ranges that surround Tucson. The hikes range from "easy" to "extremely difficult." They are grouped by mountain

1

range: nine hikes in the Tucson Mountains, five in the Rincon Mountains, eleven in the Santa Catalina Mountains, and eight in the Santa Rita Mountains. All are day hikes and, with the exception of two in the Santa Ritas, can be reached by passenger car.

In this project, I was aided by several people—Ruth, a good hiker and companion, who never loses her sense of humor; my daughter Cheryl, who hiked many of the Tucson Mountain trails with me and drew the maps; Shelia, who carried a leaky jug of water and a stale pizza down Mount Lemmon the day we did the Box Camp Trail; Marge, a newcomer to hiking in these parts, who still can't believe how beautiful it all is; Helen, who made the awesome trek up Pima Canyon with me; Nancy, who still speaks to me after the Pink Hill Trail; Mike, whose kind constructive comments made the third printing more accurate; and my husband, John, who puts up with it all.

Introduction

Tucson is a "hiker's heaven." To the north is the mountain range that dominates the Tucson skyline, the Santa Catalinas. Due east are the Rincons. Forty miles south of town are the Santa Rita Mountains. The Tucson Mountains to the west are the backdrop for our dramatic sunsets. Hiking is possible year round—the mild winters allow hiking in the lower elevations, and, in summer, the trails of the high mountains beckon.

To enjoy hiking in these mountains you must be properly prepared and be aware of the area's hazards. Too much exposure to the sun is dangerous. Not carrying enough water can cause serious illness or death. There are venomous creatures out there, such as rattlesnakes, scorpions, and Gila monsters. Cactus, amole, catclaw, and other thorny plants seem determined to attack you. Weather conditions can change quickly—a beautiful morning can become a stormy early afternoon.

Sounds bad! If you are properly prepared and aware of the dangers that exist, the chances of anything happening to you are remote. It is beautiful out there, and the only way you can see it is on your feet. Within a forty-five-mile radius of Tucson, the elevations go from twenty-five hundred feet to nearly ten thousand feet. Vegetation changes from cactus to scrub oak to ponderosa pine and Douglas fir. You may spot a javelina, coyote, deer, bighorn sheep, or in the highest elevations, even a bear. Hidden pools invite swimming on a hot day. The views seemingly extend forever or are limited by stark canyon walls.

This guide is intended to prepare you to hike in these mountains. The first chapter contains an inventory of proper equipment and clothing. Chapter 2 discusses what you should be aware of, such as too much sun, too little water, and those poisonous creatures. The rest of the guide is devoted to detailed descriptions of trails, divided by mountain range.

Each hike is preceded by a box of information as follows: **General Description:** a short description of the hike. **Difficulty:** I used four categories. "Easy" is a hike with minimum elevation gain or loss that nearly anyone could achieve; "moderate" is a little harder, usually over one thousand-foot elevation gain and over three miles one way; "difficult" has areas of steep elevation gain and will require most of the day; "extremely difficult" is limited to a few hikes in this guide. They require a long day, are usually over five miles one way, and are steep. **Best time of year to hike:** exactly what it says. **Length:** distance given is one way unless it is a loop hike, then the distance refers to the entire loop. **Elevation:** generally beginning and ending elevations, unless there is a high point, such as a ridge, then all three elevations are given. **Miles to trailhead from Speedway/Campbell intersection:** this is a well-known intersection in Tucson. **Directions to trailhead from Speedway/Campbell intersection:** specific directions from this intersection, which can be adapted from any place in town.

Although I have made every effort to ensure the accuracy of the trail descriptions, hiking each trail at least once and most trails two or more times, you must take the final responsibility for translating that information to your hiking boots. Heavy rains can wash out a section of a trail, or what appears to me as a distinctive landmark may mean nothing to you. Always carry this guide, a map of the area you are hiking, and a compass. Never, never hike alone. Do not overestimate your hiking ability and do not hesitate to turn back if you become disoriented. It is better to try again another day than to become a story on the evening news.

Getting Ready

Shoes. Most of the trails in the Tucson area are rocky and steep, making a sturdy hiking boot with ankle support a must. Many styles are available, from all-leather to a combination of leather and fabric. Without comfortable boots, hiking can be extremely unpleasant.

Socks. Wear two pairs—a thin inner pair and an outer pair of wool or of a wool/cotton blend.

Clothing. Wear layers. A cotton T-shirt, a lightweight long-sleeved cotton shirt, and a sweater or sweatshirt are good to start with. Lightweight long pants protect your legs from the thorny vegetation. Many hikes in the Tucson area start at a low elevation and climb several thousand feet, requiring more clothing near the end than at the beginning of the hike. Layering makes it possible to be comfortable at any elevation.

Hat. Wear a hat for protection from the sun. Many styles are available. I prefer a cotton hat with a wide brim that can be tossed in the washer after a few wearings.

Walking Stick. In the rough terrain around Tucson, a walking stick is helpful. Many styles are available for purchase, or you can make one of your own. I have seen several strong sticks made out of agave stalks with rubber tips on the ends to prevent splitting. Some hikers use ski poles.

Daypack. Many styles are available. I prefer a daypack with several pockets large enough to hold some permanent supplies. Keep a first-aid kit, knife, compass, lightweight poncho, sunscreen, aspirin, and insect repellent tucked away in one pocket of the daypack. There should be room for extra bottles of water, plenty of food, and a warm jacket. A daypack the size kids use to carry books is perfect.

Canteen. Many types of canteens are available. Whatever style you select, make sure that you keep it handy. I prefer a bottle holder that fits a belt. You'll need extra water bottles to carry in your daypack. Many hikers make do with plastic soda bottles or hospital IV bottles. You can also purchase all sizes and shapes of water bottles at outdoor stores.

Map. Although there are individual trail maps included in this guide, an overall map of the mountain range is helpful. United States Geological Survey maps are available for each range. The Southern Arizona Hiking Club has published helpful hiking maps of the Santa Catalina, Rincon, and Santa Rita Mountains.

Hazards of Hiking around Tucson

While hiking in the mountains around Tucson, there are three things that should be of primary concern: sun, water, and the venomous critters.

The sun shines here 360 days a year, according to the chamber of commerce. It's great for hiking and not so great for the skin.

The University of Arizona Cancer Center sponsors a Sun Awareness Project to make Tucsonans aware of the dangers of too much exposure to the sun. According to Jean Stevenson, health educator for the project, Tucson has the highest incidence of skin cancer of any place in the world, with the exception of Queensland, Australia. "Unfortunately," Stevenson explained, "for many years the idea that a tanned skin was attractive led to excessive sunbathing. Now we are seeing a dramatic increase in the incidence of skin cancer as a result."

Skin cancer is caused by the ultraviolet rays of the sun. Many geographic and meteorologic factors in Tucson combine to allow high intensities of ultraviolet radiation to reach the earth's surface. These factors include the thirty-two degree north latitude, the 2410-foot altitude, a high number of clear days, a high annual percentage of sunlight, and a high average daily temperature that encourages outdoor activity.

Despite the danger of skin cancer, it is possible to hike safely in the sun. The cardinal rule to remember is *never* hike in the Tucson area without sunscreen with a sun protection factor (SPF) of at least fifteen. Sunscreens block the ultraviolet rays. The higher the rating, the longer the rays are blocked. To see how effective your sunscreen is, check the Sun Intensity Prediction chart published daily in both Tucson newspapers. The predictions given are for untanned Caucasians, assuming no clouds, and give the total number of minutes in the sun required to redden the skin at various times during the day. The intensity varies from sixteen minutes at noon in the summer to thirty minutes at noon during the winter months. For example, if you plan to be in the sun in July at noon, it would be only sixteen minutes before your skin would redden. A sunscreen with an SPF of fifteen would lengthen the time that you could be safely exposed to the sun to four hours, or fifteen (the sun protection factor) multiplied by sixteen (the sun intensity prediction).

Many sunscreens are available. A few have an SPF as high as thirty-four. Several are water resistant. Follow instructions on the product, which usually include applying the sunscreen thirty minutes before exposure and reapplying it after swimming or heavy perspiration. Experiment and see which product suits your skin best. Today's sunscreen products are like fine lotions and have no medicinal odor.

In addition to sunscreen, the hiker should wear a wide-brimmed hat, long-sleeved cotton shirt, and lightweight long pants. Sunglasses that screen ultraviolet rays are a necessity. It is best, though usually not practical when hiking, to avoid exposure to the sun between 10:00 A.M. and 3:00 P.M. In the summer, hiking should be confined to the higher elevations because of the intensity of the sun and the extreme heat.

If you would like more detailed information, or advice on a particular sunscreen product, contact the Arizona Sun Awareness Project at 626-7935.

Water is so important in Arizona that many statutes regulate the consumption and use of water. Every summer newspapers carry accounts of death and near death from lack of water. At the least, too little water can cause headache, nausea, cramps, and fatigue. Although water consumption is especially important in summer, because of the low humidity, adequate intake is important in all seasons.

Kevin Kregel, assistant professor at the University of Arizona School for Health Related Professions, is currently researching the effects of heat stress on the thermoregulatory and cardiovascular responses, or, in laymen's terms, what happens if you don't get enough to drink.

Kregel recommends that hikers prehydrate by drinking twenty ounces of fluid two hours before hiking. During the hike take a good drink every fifteen minutes. Kregel warns: "By the time you feel thirsty, you are already slightly dehydrated." For hikes of long duration, Kregel recommends drinking a fluid replacement beverage such as Gatorade. Avoid soda pop, fruit juices, caffeinated drinks, and alcoholic beverages—all act as diuretics and cause dehydration.

One bit of good news! The idea that hikers shouldn't drink cold water is no longer accepted. According to Kregel, current research shows that cold water is absorbed into the body quicker. In fact, Kregel recommends what I have been doing for years: "Freeze it!"

Venomous critters—snakes, scorpions, and Gila monsters—are prevalent in the Sonoran Desert and in the mountains around Tucson.

Arizona reportedly has more rattlesnakes than any other state. Regardless of who's counting, Arizona rattlers have the best press agent! Rarely is there a western movie without a coiled rattler in the center of the trail. The horse rears, and our hero pulls his gun and shoots the snake between its eyes, thus averting certain disaster. In reality, rattlers present little threat to riders or hikers.

True, rattlers thrive in the canyons and mountains around Tucson. Of the eleven species of rattlers, the western diamondback is the most common and the one you are most likely to see while hiking. The western diamondback is a brownish gray with diamond-shaped markings. It has a broad triangular head, and at the end of its tail is a "rattle"—a series of connected bony segments which, when vibrated, make a sound similar to a baby's rattle.

Nancy Mellor, registered pharmacist and poison information specialist for the Arizona Poison Control Center, reports that the center receives an average of one hundred calls a year regarding rattlesnake bites. The majority of bites, according to Mellor, are "illegitimate"—that is, incurred while someone, usually a fifteen- to twenty-five-year-old male, is playing with the snake. Many of these bites involve drinking, leading the staff of the Poison Control Center to say "snakes are attracted to alcohol!" "Legitimate" bites, those suffered accidentally, are rare.

While hiking, observe a few simple precautions. Because most bites are on the extremities, do not put your hands or feet under a rock or log or any other place a snake might be sleeping. Never sit down without looking. Wear sturdy hiking boots that cannot be penetrated by fangs, and wear long pants to slow the effect of a bite. If you see a snake, assume that it is poisonous and give it a wide berth. If you hear a rattle, stop immediately, determine the location of the snake, and get away from it.

If you or someone in your hiking party should be bitten, the single most important thing you can do, according to Mellor, is to remain calm and seek medical care. Mellor adds, "Your best defense is your car keys."

Some specialists are beginning to cautiously recommend use of an extractor, an inexpensive device that uses a vacuum suction to extract venom. Mellor advises that the kit must be used immediately after the bite and that the cup that receives the blood must be continuously emptied. The Poison Control Center is not officially recommending use of the kit until more studies are conducted.

The center does recommend applying a wide constricting band between the bite and the heart, making sure that the band is loose enough so that a finger can be inserted between it and the limb. If possible, immobilize the limb with a splint or sling.

Until recently, experts recommended cutting across the bite and sucking the venom. Mellor advises *never* to cut a snake bite. More damage can be caused by the cut than by the bite. Other don'ts are: never apply ice to the bite area; do not give alcohol; and do not waste time catching the snake because today's antivenins are effective against all pit vipers, regardless of kind.

Scorpions also unnecessarily strike fear into the hearts of hikers. Of the thirty species of scorpions in Arizona, only one, the bark scorpion, is poisonous. Although chances of a fatality from a scorpion bite are remote (no deaths have occurred in Arizona in thirty years), caution should be observed. Scorpions spend the daylight hours under cover and emerge only at night, and then only when the nighttime lows exceed 77 degrees. The bark scorpion never burrows and is most commonly found in riparian areas such as desert canyons and groves of mesquite, cottonwood, and Arizona sycamore. The bark scorpion could bite if it is disturbed by a hiker leaning on a tree or moving a log. Although the bark scorpion can be distinguished from other species, any scorpion bite should be taken seriously. If possible, capture the scorpion so it can be determined if it is the bark scorpion.

First aid treatment for a scorpion bite is to get to a medical facility as soon as possible. If you cannot reach medical assistance within thirty minutes, apply a loose constricting band between the bite and the heart.

The Gila monster also has a good press agent. This lizard is a brilliantly colored black and yellow or black and pink creature, so rare that it is protected by Arizona state law. Legend has it that once a Gila monster bites, it will not release its victim until it thunders! While Gila monsters are the only lizard in the United States whose bite is poisonous, danger to hikers is negligible. They are rarely seen in the wild. If one is seen at all it is usually at dusk, or after a summer rain in a canyon bottom where the lizard has access to moist soil. To get bitten while hiking you would practically have to fall near one and surprise it. The overwhelming majority of bites have occurred by handling captive Gila monsters.

Should you or a member of your party get bitten by a Gila monster, you don't have to wait until it thunders. A Gila monster will, however, hold on for at least fifteen minutes, during which time venom is pouring into the wound. The first thing to do is release the Gila monster's jaws from the bite so as to lessen the amount of venom injected into the body. A strong stick between the jaws usually works. If this is ineffective, the Gila monster may be encouraged to release its grip by placing an open flame under its jaw. Immersing the extremity and the Gila monster under water will work. If neither a stick, flame, nor water is available, grab the Gila monster by the tail and jerk. This will cause more damage to the wound, but anything is better than letting the lizard retain its grip.

First aid involves letting the wound bleed freely for several minutes while flushing with water. Apply a constricting band between the wound and the heart. Immobilize the limb and seek medical help as soon as possible.

Further information and advice is available twenty-four hours a day from the Arizona Poison Control Center. In Tucson call 626-6016. Outside of the Tucson calling area, call 1-800-362-0101.

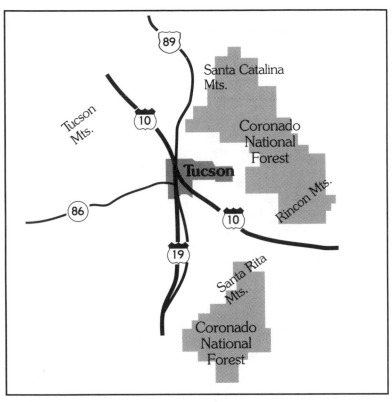

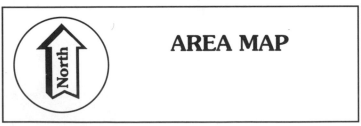

AREA MAP

The Tucson Mountains

Tucson's sunsets are one of our city's trademarks. The mountains silhouetted on postcards are the Tucson Mountains, the smallest of the four ranges that surround Tucson. The high point, Wasson Peak at 4,687 feet, is barely a mountain by most standards.

The Tucson Mountains are different in character from other ranges. No ponderosa pine will shade your path while hiking here. This is the land of mesquite and palo verde, of the saguaro, prickly pear, cholla, and hedgehog cactus, of the creosote bush, ocotillo, and catclaw. The terrain is a jumble of boulders and craggy ridges.

From A.D. 900 to 1300, the Hohokam lived in the river bottoms in their pit houses and hunted in the Tucson Mountains. Petroglyphs in Kings Canyon and Picture Rocks remain as evidence of their existence. The Hohokam were gone when Father Kino first came to the Tucson area in 1692. By then the Pima were living at the base of the mountain we now call "A" Mountain.

The Tucson Mountains were significant in the early history of Tucson. In 1772 King Carlos II of Spain, who possessed this land on paper, issued an order calling for the reorganization of the presidios (forts) in Mexico and the Southwest. The site selected for a new presidio was a point near the Santa Cruz River opposite the Pima village at the base of Sentinel Mountain (now commonly called "A" Mountain). Construction began in 1776, but progress was slow, and it was not until December of 1783 that the task was completed. A lookout was maintained on top of Sentinel Peak, and the fort was warned when the Apaches swept down out of the Santa Catalinas or Rincons. Several attacks were withstood, and the town of Tucson outgrew the walls of the fort by the mid-1800s; Sentinel Peak was no longer needed as a lookout.

The mountain did serve other purposes. Many early Tucson homes and even the wall around the University of Arizona were built from black rock quarried from the side of Sentinel Peak.

Copper was discovered in the 1870s at Silver Bell, and mining became important. Hikers in the Tucson Mountains today can see much evidence of early mining. The Sendero Esperanza Trail passes the old Gould Mine, once thought to be the bonanza of the territory. The Hugh Norris Trail passes several mines. The Starr Pass Trail follows the route of a shortcut through the mountains to the mines of Quijotoa. From the ridges and peaks you can still see operating copper mines.

As late as the 1920s and 1930s the land in the Tucson Mountains was open to homesteading. A stone house remains on the David Yetman Trail that was homesteaded in 1930 by a newspaper man from Illinois. Ranchers ran cattle in the mountains.

It seemed that the Tucson Mountains were open for grabs. Mining, cattle grazing, and homesteading were being carried on with little regard for the ecology of the mountains; that is until Pima County agricultural agent C. B. Brown took it upon himself to preserve the Tucson Mountain area. With the help of Senator Carl Hayden, Brown was able to persuade Congress to withdraw sixty thousand acres from the Homesteading Act of 1873 to create Tucson Mountain Park.

World War I veterans complained that their rights were being violated as they could not homestead, and as a result all but 28,988 acres were turned back over to the U.S. Department of Interior to be used for homesteading. On 11 April 1929 this remaining acreage was designated as Tucson Mountain Park. The Pima County Parks Commission was established, and Brown was named chairman.

The area was still not pristine and secure from development. Mining was still permitted on much of the land. In 1939 Columbia Pictures leased three hundred acres of state land within the park for movie production and built the Old Tucson Studios. In one movie, six acres of desert were set on fire, completely destroying all vegetation, including several mature saguaros. Public uproar caused the Pima County Parks Commission to purchase the lease from Columbia Pictures, establishing control and assuring that no fires would be set in the desert again.

In 1952 Arthur Pack, a member of the Parks Commission, decided that it would be appropriate to start a museum within Tucson Mountain Park that would educate the public as to the Sonoran Desert, and the world famous Arizona-Sonora Desert Museum was formed. This excellent facility competes with the Grand Canyon as the most visited attraction in Arizona.

In 1961 President John Kennedy added 15,360 acres of federally owned land in Tucson Mountain Park to the Saguaro National Monument to be administered by the National Park Service. This change of jurisdiction was made specifically to prevent mining claims in the area and to preserve the natural beauty. Because of this move, the Tucson Mountain Park was reduced to 13,628 acres. The trails that converge on Wasson Peak are now within the Saguaro National Monument and are managed by the National Park Service.

An additional three thousand acres were added to the park in 1974 as a result of a bond election. Were it not for the efforts of many concerned citizens, beginning with C. B. Brown, much of the Tucson Mountains would be developed today, mined and bulldozed beyond recognition. Fortunately, much of the area is preserved and accessible to hikers.

As you will see in the following descriptions, the trails in the Tucson Mountains are not difficult. Several are rated "easy." A good introduction to this area is to hike the David Yetman Trail using a two-car shuttle. The Hugh Norris Trail to the summit of Wasson Peak is the most difficult trail but the one that provides the best views of the Tucson area. These mountains are ideal for winter hiking and cool early spring and late fall days. By summer it is way too hot.

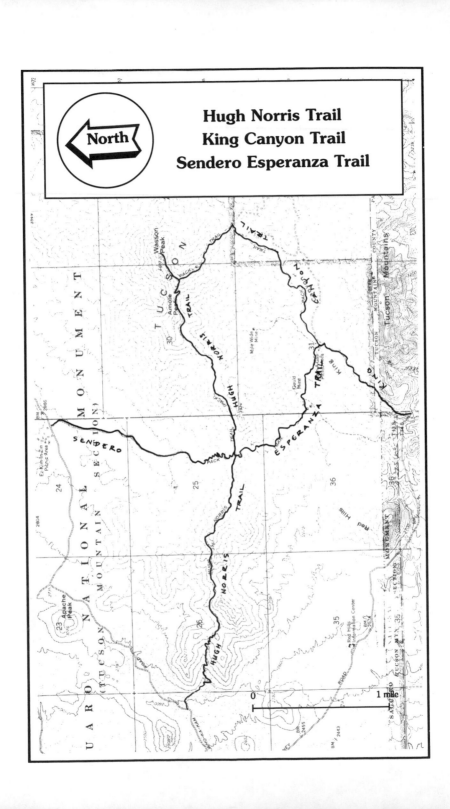

Hugh Norris Trail
King Canyon Trail
Sendero Esperanza Trail

Hugh Norris Trail

General Description

> A pleasant ridge ramble past old mines to the highest peak in the Tucson Mountains

Difficulty

> Moderate, some areas of steep switchbacks

Best time of year to hike

> Winter

Length

> 4.9 miles from trailhead to Wasson Peak

Elevation

> 2600 feet at the trailhead; 4687 feet at Wasson Peak

Miles to trailhead from Speedway/Campbell intersection

> 19

Directions to trailhead from Speedway/Campbell intersection

> Go west on Speedway 11.8 miles to the intersection with Kinney Road. (Note: At the intersection of Anklam Road, Speedway becomes Gates Pass Road.) Turn right on Kinney Road, following the signs to the Saguaro National Monument. The entrance to the monument is signed and is to the right. Drive past the Red Hills Information Center to the Bajada Loop Drive, which is well marked. The Hugh Norris trailhead is .8 miles ahead on unpaved road. There is a small parking area on the right.

My favorite route to the summit of Wasson Peak is the Hugh Norris Trail. Although longer than other routes, the climb is gradual and the views from the ridges are spectacular. Wasson Peak offers an unforgettable 360-degree view of the Tucson Valley.

This excellent trail is named for Hugh Norris, a Tohono O'odham Indian police chief. The peak it reaches was named for John Wasson, a colorful, often controversial early editor of the *Tucson Citizen,* who much to his surprise was appointed surveyor general of the Arizona Territory in 1870. Although he had absolutely no experience in the field, he retained the position until 1882 when he moved to California.

Tucson from Wasson Peak, Hugh Norris Trail

Signs at the beginning of the Hugh Norris Trail are typical of the trailheads in the Saguaro National Monument West. Pets are prohibited, as are bicycles, motor vehicles, and weapons. A map depicts the trails of the monument, listing the distances in miles and kilometers. There is also a trail register. It's fun to read the register and note where the hikers came from, especially in winter when people converge on Tucson from all over the United States and the world. These registers serve other purposes. The rangers can judge trail usage, and if a search and rescue operation is necessary, searchers can tell if the lost hiker did indeed go on this trail. A final sign indicates that the trailhead elevation is twenty-six hundred feet.

The trail climbs gradually at first and then becomes steeper. The only difficulty is stepping over the rocks placed across the trail to prevent erosion. After about a quarter of a mile, the trail crosses a deep,sandy drainage, climbs out, and heads up the canyon directly between two ridges. As you gain elevation, look back at the saguaro forest. There is no place like this in the world. Thousands of giant saguaro spread across the bajada. Beyond the saguaros are the farms of Avra Valley. What appears to be a very straight road across the edge of the farm area is actually the canal of the Central

Arizona Project, which delivers water from the Colorado River to Phoenix and Tucson.

As the drainage narrows, the trail steepens and becomes a series of switchbacks that lead to the top of the ridge. To the north, where the walls of the drainage provide protection for the tiny saguaro seeds, there are many young saguaro. This is a pretty, quiet area. The sounds of planes overhead and the occasional pecking of a woodpecker or chirping of other birds is all you hear. You can easily reach the top of this first ridge in forty-five minutes.

On top of the ridge the trail turns to the right and is level, then quickly turns left and gradually switchbacks to the top of a small saddle. In this saddle there are several side paths that lead to the viewpoints on both sides of the saddle where there are many boulders that make a good lunch or snack spot.

From this saddle the trail descends briefly, crosses a longer saddle, and begins a long trek along the north side of the ridge. This is a very pleasant portion of the trail. There is some slight elevation gain, but nothing serious. The trail is now basically a ridge trail, meandering from one side of the ridge to the other and occasionally going along the top. The views change from one side to the other, first the Catalinas, then Picacho Peak, then the Santa Ritas or Rincons. Below and to the northwest, the Sendero Esperanza Trail winds its way through the basin and up the ridge. Far to the north and high on the ridge you can see where the Hugh Norris Trail continus its climb to Wasson Peak.

After leveling out on top of the ridge, the trail passes a fenced mine to the right. This is not a deep shaft and is most likely a prospector's pit (called a gopher's hole by the miners), dug to see what ore was under the surface. A few more yards along the trail there is a more extensive mine that has a deep shaft and a tunnel. This could be very dangerous, yet there are signs of where people have crawled under the fence to explore just a little farther, a dangerous practice that has led to the loss of several lives in the Tucson Mountains. A half of a mile past the pit and around the east side of the ridge is a signed trail intersection.

This is a good resting spot and meeting place for people who have arranged car swaps to prevent the retracing of steps. For example, one car can be left at the Sendero Esperanza trailhead, another at Hugh Norris, and still another at King Canyon. All hikers can converge on Wasson Peak and return by a different route. The Hugh Norris Trail continues straight past the intersection and along the ridge for 2.7 miles to the summit of Wasson Peak.

From the intersection it is a gradual climb along the northwestern side of the ridge. As on the first section of the trail, the rocks placed on the trail for erosion control are the only problem. After half a mile, the trail crosses a short saddle from which the hiker can see both sides of the mountain. As you look ahead to the peaks, it is difficult to figure out which one is actually Wasson. It is not the one it appears to be, but the peak farthest away and to the left. After the saddle the trail crosses back to the western side of the ridge. At a small sign marking the four thousand-foot elevation level, the trail turns to the right and quickly left across another short saddle, following the east side of the ridge along a smooth, sandy trail.

The trail from this point again meanders from one side of the ridge to the other, interspersed with small saddles. It is smooth and not at all difficult. From this portion of the trail you can see more extensive evidence of the mining that took place in the Tucson Mountains in the early 1900s and again in the 1940s.

Most of the last half-mile of the trail is a series of steep switchbacks. The large rock outcropping directly ahead of the switchbacks is not Wasson Peak, as you will shortly realize, although from the switchbacks it appears to be the high point. At the top of the switchbacks it is a signed trail intersection. The King Canyon trailhead is 3.2 miles down the other side of the ridge. The Hugh Norris Trail continues an easy .3 miles to the summit.

Right before the summit is a trail sign-in box. It is interesting to read the comments of hikers when they reach this vantage point. People from all over the United States have signed the trail registers with comments such as "Better than Mount Rainier!," "A fantastic day," and frequently just "Wow!" On a clear day you can see all of Tucson and the surrounding mountains. The comments are understandable.

King Canyon Trail

General Description

A hike up a canyon past petroglyphs and old mines to the intersection of the Hugh Norris Trail near the top of Wasson Peak

Difficulty

Moderate, short areas of moderate climbing

Best time of year to hike

Winter

Length

3.5 miles to intersection with Hugh Norris Trail

Elevation

2800 feet at the trailhead; 4600 feet at trail intersection

Miles to trailhead from Speedway/Campbell intersection

14.6

Directions to trailhead from Speedway/Campbell intersection

Go west on Speedway, over Gates Pass to the intersection with Kinney Road. Turn right on Kinney Road to the Arizona-Sonora Desert Museum. The parking area for the King Canyon Trail is .1 miles past the entrance to the museum and on the right.

In 1917 the Copper King Mine was developed in this canyon. Long since abandoned, the trail up the canyon now bears the name of the mine and is known as the King Canyon Trail. In combination with the Hugh Norris Trail, the King Canyon Trail is the shortest route to the summit of Wasson Peak.

Signs at the trailhead warn about the open mine shafts. A sign also notes that one quart of water is the minimum that the hiker should carry to hike this trail. On warm days one quart is not enough. It is better to have more water than necessary. The sign also indicates that King Canyon has the only permanent source of water in the Tucson Mountains; there is a spring, but it is hard to locate.

The trail begins as an old jeep road and for the first mile is a wide, rocky walk along the west side of the ridge. Most of the year

Petroglyphs—Hohokam Indians, 900 A.D.-1300 A.D. King Canyon Trail

the canyon drainage is dry, but in times of heavy rain the rush of water would be an awesome sight. Soon you can see the picnic shelter of the Mam-a-Gah picnic area and the rock building that serves as a restroom below it.

As the road approaches the intersection, it drops into and crosses the canyon. Off the trail and to the left, about one-quarter of a mile down the canyon drainage and immediately past a small dam, are many petroglyphs. On both sides of the drainage are etched drawings that were made by Hohokam Indians who lived in these mountains from A.D. 900 to 1300. Some of the drawings are intricate, and others look like a child's scribbling. If you are hiking just the King Canyon Trail, you can save this exploration for the return trip because the wash can be followed almost to the highway, where a path leads up to the parking lot. If you are trading keys with a fellow hiker and will not return by this route, it is worth the short side trip to see the petroglyphs.

As you cross the canyon bottom, a short side trail to the left leads up to the Mam-a-Gah picnic area, where there are six tables and one ramada. This frequently used picnic area is named for the "deer dance" of the Tohono O'odham Indians. The King Canyon

Trail turns to the right, past the restrooms. The Sendero Esperanza trailhead is immediately past the restroom and to the left. King Canyon Trail is straight ahead and, as the sign indicates, reaches Wasson Peak in 2.6 miles.

Past the intersection the trail narrows and continues up the canyon. No longer a jeep road, the trail is now very rocky, and sturdy hiking boots are a necessity. In about two hundred yards the trail crosses another drainage, and it then goes along a low ridge between King Canyon and the side drainage for a short distance before beginning to climb. To the east is an old mine road built when hope was high for the mining potential in these mountains.

The Mile Wide Mining Company owned the claims in this area, and geologist reports were optimistic. Charles F. Willis, geologist and editor of the *Arizona Mining Journal,* said in August of 1916 that "the Mile Wide Copper Company is destined to become one of the large producers for which the State of Arizona is so well known . . . the property has everything pointing toward success and absolutely none of the sign boards of failure." The company named their main mine the Copper King, lowering shafts to a depth of four hundred feet and excavating tunnels. Mining was carried out in 1917 and 1918 and again briefly in 1943, but it was never the hoped-for success. The Copper King passed through several owners before being abandoned altogether, achieving a total production of only fourteen hundred tons. All that remains today are the scars.

The trail continues to climb along the east side of the hill and is easy to follow. In about one mile it reaches the top of the ridge and again becomes an abandoned road. If you are hiking here in early spring, which arrives in late February, this area is usually dotted with wildflowers. If the rains have been sufficient and the winter not too cold, tiny golden poppies peek through the rocks. Look closely and you will see other flowers. It is one of the mysteries of nature that these flowers can survive the harsh conditions that exist in these mountains.

The road winds around the side of the hill and comes to the intersection with the Sweetwater Trail. Because there is no legal public access to the Sweetwater Trail, the Park Service recommends that you go down and return from this intersection. Now, for the first time on the King Canyon Trail, you can see the other side of the mountain and the western end of the Santa Catalina range. It is now only 1.2 miles to Wasson Peak; however, it is a steep 1.2 miles.

From this intersection the trail climbs steeply to the west. The main obstacles on the trail are the large rocks carefully placed to prevent erosion. The peak directly above you is not Wasson. The trail becomes a series of switchbacks that climb steadily. There are several fenced mine shafts along this portion of the trail, all with warning signs. As you switchback up the trail, more mines become visible, some in places that look totally inaccessible. You wonder why that particular site was chosen, as the terrain is so rugged and barren.

As the trail reaches the top of the switchbacks, most of the city is visible, and Wasson Peak stands out to the north. As the trail levels along the north side of the ridge, you can see the trail intersection sign ahead. Another fenced mine is on the right, this time with the warning sign in Spanish: Peligro Excavacion. Past this mine, the trail is level briefly and then climbs in a few switchbacks to the trail intersection. This is the end of the King Canyon Trail. To reach Wasson Peak, follow the Hugh Norris Trail .3 miles to the summit. The final section is easy and well worth the brief climb required.

Sendero Esperanza Trail

General Description

    A short trail across a ridge, with great views in all directions

Difficulty

    Moderate, some areas of steep switchbacks

Best time of year to hike

    Winter

Length

    3.2 miles

Elevation

    2800 feet at Golden Gate Road trailhead; 3633 feet at intersection with Hugh Norris Trail; 3200 feet at intersection with King Canyon Trail

Miles to trailhead from Speedway/Campbell intersection

    22.2

Directions to trailhead from Speedway/Campbell intersection

    Go west on Speedway, over Gates Pass, until the intersection with Kinney Road. Turn right on Kinney Road, past the Arizona-Sonora Desert Museum and the Red Hills Information Center. Turn right on Bajada Loop Drive. The Loop Drive is unpaved and becomes one way after the Hugh Norris trailhead. Turn right on Golden Gate Road to the parking area for the Sendero Esperanza trailhead.

    Esperanza is Spanish for "hope," thus *sendero esperanza* is the "trail of hope." How this name came to be attached to the trail is unclear, but one can speculate that, since the trail leads to a large mine, someone once hoped to find riches at the end of the trail!

    The Sendero Esperanza Trail climbs the ridge directly to the east of the trailhead and descends the other side, past the extensive workings of the old Gould Mine, ending at the intersection of the King Canyon Trail one mile north of the Arizona-Sonora Desert Museum. At 1.8 miles the Sendero Esperanza Trail intersects with the Hugh Norris Trail and makes an excellent route to the top of Wasson Peak. From the parking area to Wasson Peak, the total mileage is 4.0 miles.

Powder House—Gould Mine, Sendero Esperanza Trail

Signs at the parking area give a detailed map of the trail system. Pay careful attention to the Open Mine Shafts—Please Stay on Trail warning. There are many abandoned mine shafts in the area, and lives have been lost by curious explorers who just couldn't resist one more step.

The Sendero Esperanza Trail is flat and sandy for almost the first mile as it follows a drainage and gains elevation gradually. After the first mile, the trail narrows and turns gradually to the right for a short distance before beginning to climb the switchbacks to the left.

As you look toward the mountain, you can see the ridge that you are about to climb. As you begin to climb the switchbacks, the trail becomes quite rocky in places. The views to the north and northwest are great on a clear day. You can see the mines of the Cyprus Copper Company. The mountain without a top is the limestone quarry for the Portland Cement Company. It is gradually getting smaller, as you will see if you hike this trail again in ten years. Depending on the time of year, the fields near Marana are squares of green or brown. The triangular outline of Picacho Peak stands out forty miles north of Tucson. Now a state park, the peak stands in history, a bit erroneously, as the site of the westernmost battle of the Civil War.

As you top the ridge, you come to the well-marked intersection of the Hugh Norris and Sendero Esperanza trails. From this vantage point, you can see the Red Hills Information Center, the traffic on Kinney Road, and the Santa Rita Mountains to the south. Mount Wrightson and Mount Hopkins are the dominant peaks in this range. The Sendero Esperanza Trail drops to the other side of the ridge, past the Mam-a-Gah picnic area, to intersect with the King Canyon Trail.

The trail descends immediately down the west side of the ridge. It is quite rocky and can be treacherous as it switchbacks and curves downward quickly. This rocky portion is short, and after a quarter of a mile, the trail intersects with an old mine road. The Sendero Esperanza Trail goes to the left. The old road is smooth and easy to walk on. It remains level or a very gradual downhill for a quarter of a mile or so. There are abandoned mines along the trail. These mines were operated in the days before environmental protection was an issue, so there are many scars.

The views from the road are excellent. Kitt Peak and Baboquivari Mountain stand out in the distance. To the west the hills made red by iron oxide are distinct. There are many old weather-beaten saguaro along the road.

Near the bottom of the hill is the old Gould Copper Mine. The *Arizona Daily Star* carried enthusiastic reports of the potential of the mine, stating on 17 May 1905 that the "Gould people talk as if they have the biggest bonanza in the territory." By 21 December reports were that the "Gould was working day and night." On 7 July 1907 the *Star* reported "15 wagons carrying ore from the Gould Mine to the Southern Pacific for shipment to El Paso." The Gould Mine worked at a depth of 360 feet and was in production intermittently from 1905 until 1912. Despite the optimism, the total production of the Gould Mine was only fifteen hundred tons. The owners were forced into bankruptcy in 1915. A fenced shaft partially covered by boards, a few old beams on the side of the hill, and, one hundred yards past the mine, a stone powder house are all that remain of the Gould Mine today.

Right past the mine, the road crosses a deep drainage that runs immediately after a rain. On both sides of the drainage there is evidence of other mines. Across the drainage the trail climbs gradually. As you round the bend, the shelter and picnic tables of the Mam-a-Gah picnic area are visible. This is a popular destination for hikers entering from the King Canyon trailhead. As the trail crosses a small drainage you will notice an unmarked path to the right that leads to the picnic area. The trail continues straight ahead, and in about two hundred yards you will come to the official signed path that leads up to the picnic tables. The Sendero Esperanza Trail ends two hundred yards past this sign.

A sign indicates that the Arizona-Sonora Desert Museum is one mile ahead. The King Canyon trailhead is .9 miles along the road across the wash. There are restrooms to the right. If you are doing a key swap, continue on the King Canyon Trail to the parking area; otherwise, return to the Sendero Esperanza trailhead by retracing your steps.

David Yetman Trail

General Description
An easy walk through typical vegetation of the Sonoran Desert
Difficulty
Easy, few areas with slight elevation gain
Best time of year to hike
Winter
Length
5.4 miles
Elevation
3000 feet from Gates Pass trailhead; 2700 feet at Camino de Oeste
Miles to trailhead from Speedway/Campbell intersection
10.1 to parking area on west side of Gates Pass
Directions to trailhead from Speedway/Campbell intersection
The Yetman Trail has two trailheads. It is possible to leave cars at each trailhead and work out combinations that enable you not to have to retrace steps. A good combination that makes the most of the hike downhill is to leave a vehicle at the Camino de Oeste trailhead and continue to the Gates Pass trailhead. To do this go west on Speedway. Shortly after passing the West Anklam Road-Speedway intersection, turn left on Camino de Oeste. Drive as far as you can up the unpaved road and leave a car. Continue on Speedway, which is now called Gates Pass Road, across Gates Pass and down the west side of the mountain to a large parking area on the left almost at the bottom of the mountain. This is the starting point for the David Yetman and Golden Gate trails.

David Yetman was a member of the Pima County Board of Supervisors from 1977 to 1988. Sometimes controversial, Yetman became known for his fervent defense of the environment. The Yetman Trail, which crosses a lovely area in the Tucson Mountains, was named in his honor when he retired from the board of supervisors.

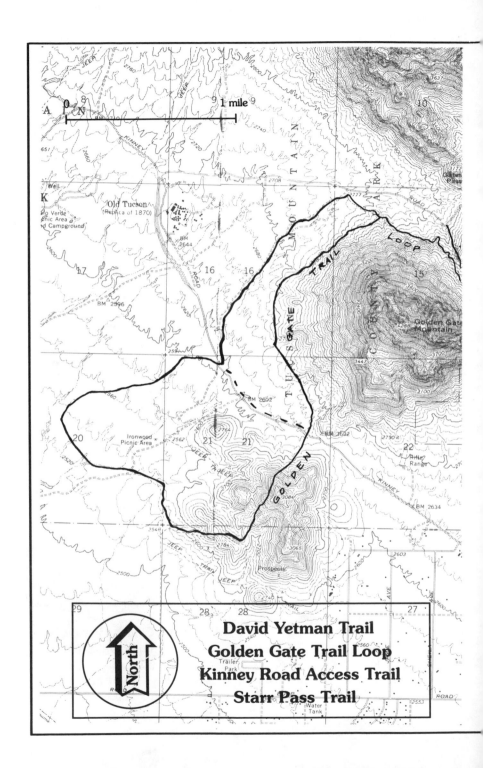

David Yetman Trail
Golden Gate Trail Loop
Kinney Road Access Trail
Starr Pass Trail

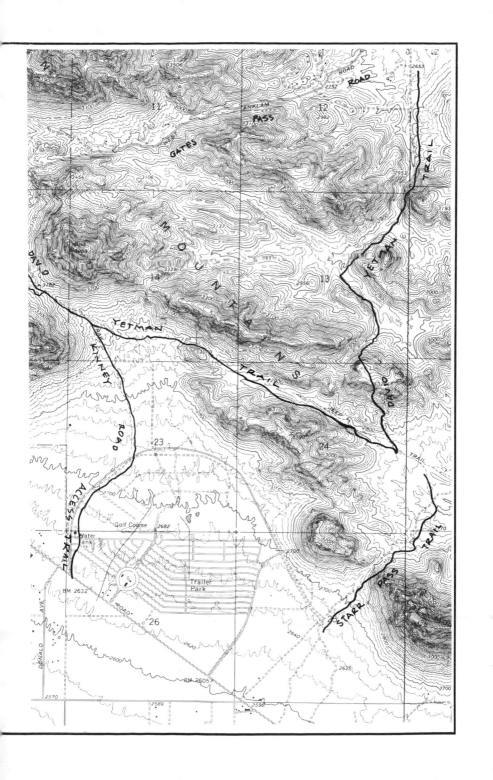

Sherry and Ruby Bowen homestead, David Yetman Trail

The David Yetman Trail is marked by a sign on the left. The trail begins on an old mine or jeep road. It goes between two peaks and is at first a gradual incline before leveling off. After .5 miles, signs indicate the intersection of three trails—the Golden Gate Trail to the right, the Gates Pass Trail to the left, and the David Yetman Trail straight ahead.

The Yetman Trail goes through the pass and continues downhill. This is an easy trail and is perfect for people who want to become better acquainted with the Sonoran Desert without too much elevation gain. This portion goes through lots of teddy bear cholla and is very smooth. After about .5 miles a sign indicates that the Yetman Trail bears to the left. This portion of the trail is well marked as it meanders in and out of small drainages.

After approximately one mile, the trail crosses a deep wash and climbs briefly, albeit steeply, to the side of a ridge. The side of the hill to the left of the wash protects an excellent stand of saguaro.

The trail continues along the side of the hill for a short distance before descending into a creek bed. For nearly a mile the trail follows the usually dry creek bed, crossing occasionally from one side to the other.

The trail leaves the creek and emerges from the hills and is now in the open. It is wide and sandy; in fact, it is almost a road. Signs and sounds of civilization begin to appear—a telephone line, the sound of automobiles. Signs indicate the intersection of the David Yetman and Starr Pass trails. Continue to the left on the David Yetman Trail.

You quickly come to a sign pointing to the Thirty-sixth Street trailhead .9 miles ahead, a popular access for mountain bikers. The Yetman Trail goes past the sign, to the left, along an old jeep road. The road drops into a wash and begins a gradual climb uphill. At the top of the hill a trail sign indicates that the Yetman trailhead is 1.6 miles to the left.

The trail now becomes narrow and divides to go around a large palo verde tree. It quickly joins and begins to parallel the fence boundary of Tucson Mountain Park. As you climb, the construction to the right of the trail is clearly visible. This is a water storage facility for the Central Arizona Project (CAP) which began operation in 1992. More CAP construction is visible from the Starr Pass and Kinney Road Access trails that connect with the David Yetman Trail. Also visible from this section of the trail is the downtown Tucson area and the Catalina Mountains. There is an unusual number of young saguaros along the east side of the ridge, probably one hundred or more in the fifteen-to twenty-five-year-old range. The trail is narrow, has lots of loose rocks, and climbs rather steeply to the top of the ridge where the other side of the mountain, including Gates Pass, is visible.

This is a very pleasant part of the trail. It goes gently downhill through a level valley. There is no sign of civilization, and it is very peaceful. In early spring there is a scattering of Mexican poppies and other wildflowers. Small trail signs indicate the correct route, which now drops into a creekbed, whose sandy bottom makes for more difficult walking.

A short way down the wash, a path leads out of the wash to a stone house that is clearly visible from the trail. This house is built of native stone and at one time suffered fire damage. There is no roof; only the sturdy walls remain.

The house was built in the early thirties by Sherry Bowen, a typesetter and, later, city editor for the *Arizona Daily Star*. Bowen brought his wife, Ruby, to Tucson from Rockford, Illinois, in the late twenties, hoping that the climate would help her serious heart condition. They lived first in Tucson, but soon homesteaded in the

Tucson Mountains, eventually owning two thousand acres. They moved to the homestead in 1931, living in a cabin while the house was built.

Ruby Bowen kept a diary of her first year in the Tucson Mountains. She wrote of the wild mountain sheep that came to the base of the cliffs nearly every evening to graze and then majestically climbed the steep canyon walls to return to a cave that was their home. A mountain lion would pace about when she was cooking meat and one time attempted to get in the window. Javelina, deer, and even a herd of wild horses came into their canyon.

The recuperative powers of the desert worked. The Bowen's daughter was born in 1943. They left Tucson in 1944 for New York City, where Sherry Bowen worked for the Associated Press. The valley and their homestead became part of Tucson Mountain Park in 1983.

The trail passes to the left of the Bowen house, crosses the creek, and again follows the creek bed, now wide and sandy. To the left is a partially covered well. Toss a rock down the well and it will eventually hit water. Now very dangerous because the covering can be easily moved, this well is scheduled to become a wildlife watering tank.

The trail follows the wide creekbed to the trailhead. On the left side there are hundreds of healthy saguaros. The creekbed in early spring is covered with an assortment of wildflowers. The trailhead marks the boundary of the Tucson Mountain Park. To reach your car at Camino de Oeste you must walk on a dirt road through privately owned land.

Golden Gate Trail Loop

General Description
An easy hike around the mountain used as the backdrop in many western movies

Difficulty
Easy, few areas with moderate elevation gain

Best time of year to hike
Winter, late fall, early spring

Length
6.6 miles for loop; add 2.1 to Ironwood picnic area

Elevation
3182 feet at trailhead; 2620 feet at Kinney Road

Miles to trailhead from Speedway/Campbell intersection
10.1

Directions to trailhead from Speedway/Campbell intersection
Go west on Speedway, over Gates Pass to the parking area on the left near the bottom of the mountain. (Past Anklam Road, Speedway becomes Gates Pass Road.) This is the trailhead for the David Yetman Trail. The Golden Gate trailhead is .5 miles along the Yetman Trail.

The Golden Gate Trail Loop circles Golden Gate Mountain. Legend has it that the mountain was so named because early prospectors thought Gates Pass and the mountain was the gate to the gold in the Tucson Mountains.

Whatever the reason for the name, it is a beautiful trail and can be hiked in combination with other trails in the area to form a loop to return to the parking lot. As is true of most trails in the Tucson Mountains, the Golden Gate Trail Loop is basically a desert ramble. At first the desert appears barren, but with experience you learn to look for the small things—the colorful lizard scurrying out of your way, the magenta bloom of a hedgehog cactus in spring, the teddy bear cholla glistening in the sun. The desert is a special place and one that you will learn to appreciate as you hike the trails.

From the parking area, proceed up the David Yetman Trail for about .5 miles to a signed intersection. The Golden Gate Trail

Golden Gate Mountain, Golden Gate Trail Loop

is to the right. It is well constructed and easy to follow.

At first the trail is narrow and lined with rocks. After about one hundred yards the trail drops into and climbs out of a drainage. It heads west around the north side of the mountain, dropping in and out of drainages. In these drainages the vegetation is thicker and the area is quite pretty. After about .5 miles the trail goes downhill more steeply. It is rocky, and sturdy hiking boots are a must. One particular drainage is full of the teddy bear cholla, and if the light is right, the shiny needles make for some interesting pictures. Several of the cholla contain the intricate cone-shaped nests made by the cactus wren. These nests are works of art, fitting securely in the spiny cholla. There are very few saguaro along this first part of the trail.

The trail works its way in and out of drainages, turning first north, then south, then west again, remaining along the north side of Golden Gate Mountain. There are nice views to the west. Miles of saguaro spread out across the basin. Far in the distance you can see the buildings of the Arizona–Sonora Desert Museum. The trail alternates from being smooth to going through sections of baseball-sized rocks, all the while dropping in and out of small drainages.

Spring is the ideal time to hike in this area, when magenta hedgehog cacti, orange ocotillos, yellow prickly pears, and white saguaro blossoms make the desert a colorful place.

Many large boulders have tumbled down from Golden Gate Mountain. The terrain of the Tucson Mountains is what geologists call "chaos," a most descriptive term.

After about three quarters of a mile, the trail comes around the bend in the mountain and you can see Old Tucson Studios for the first time. Built in 1939 by Columbia Pictures for the filming of the epic outdoor western, *Arizona*, the set has been home to many westerns over the years, such as *Gunfight at the O.K. Corral, Rio Bravo, Cimarron,* and *Three Amigos.* In later years the television series "Gunsmoke," "High Chaparral," and "Bonanza" were filmed in the area. More recently "Young Riders" has seen action at Old Tucson Studios.

The trail shortly goes down the side of the mountain and heads west along the flat basin. As you pass a huge pile of boulders on the left, the trail divides and becomes, for the first time, confusing. Turn left toward the rocks, but do not continue past the rocks. Instead, turn right. A line of rocks marks the trail that you should use. Other trails lead to the boulders and beyond, but the Golden Gate Trail is clearly marked and goes to the west, almost immediately crossing a small drainage.

For most of this part of the trail you can see Old Tucson Studios. The trail is now level and is easy, pleasant walking. To the left are excellent views of Golden Gate Mountain. After one-quarter of a mile you come to an intersection. Again, you should continue straight ahead along the trail that is marked by a line of rocks. As you circle Golden Gate Mountain, you go in and out of several small drainages. Again there are patches of cholla. This is a popular route for horseback riders and occasionally a mountain biker. It is a peaceful section and, although you are clearly near civilization and tour buses, it seems that you are alone in the desert.

The trail continues southwest, away from Old Tucson Studios, and soon you can no longer see the movie set. Most of the hikes in the Tucson Mountains lead to the tops of mountains. It is a good change to be down in the basin looking up. Baboquivari and Kitt Peak are clearly visible. For a short distance you can see Mount Wrightson to the south. As the trail nears the road, it becomes very flat and smooth. Soon you come upon signs reading Pack It Out and No Fires. At the road a small sign indicates Trail. This is Kinney Road, and in the tourist season it can be very busy. Beside the Trail sign is a large parking area with a yellow gate. At this point you have hiked 1.9 miles.

Here you have several alternatives. Across the road you can see a trail sign. This is Prospector's Trail, which can be used to make a loop around the Ironwood picnic area, past Old Tucson Studios, and back to the Golden Gate Trail. You can also walk a short distance on the right side of Kinney Road to the next parking area and take the trail past Old Tucson Studios to return to the Golden Gate Trail. Or you can retrace your steps on the Golden Gate Trail.

I recommend walking along Kinney Road to the next parking area, a distance of .4 miles. Again, there is a parking area with a yellow entrance gate and a sign that reads Trail. This is an easy, pleasant walk along an old road, with Old Tucson Studios on the left and Golden Gate Mountain on the right. After about three-quarters of a mile, the road narrows into a trail, again lined with rocks.

As the trail circles away from Golden Gate Mountain and heads toward Gates Pass Road, you know that you will soon be able to turn to the right and rejoin the Golden Gate Trail. The best route is to continue on the trail, which by now is a road again, toward Gates Pass Road, and then take an old jeep road to the right. The jeep road is about two hundred yards from the highway. This old section of road quickly joins a wider road that comes in from Gates Pass Road. Follow this road across a wide drainage to a fork. Again go right. Now you should recognize the large pile of rocks where the trail forked and first became confusing. This is where you rejoin the Golden Gate Trail, which goes to the left. The trail is easily recognizable because it is lined with rocks. Follow this trail back to the parking area. It is .3 miles long and is uphill in places. As you near the parking area you can see your car, and it is tempting to bushwack down into the ravine and scramble up the side to the car. Having tried this, I can advise that it is much easier to follow the trail to the Yetman Trail intersection and return to the parking lot down the wide road.

If you want a longer hike, a second alternative is to cross Kinney Road and take the Prospector's Trail. This route will add 2.1 miles to your hike. I did not find the area that scenic or interesting, except for the first portion that is Prospector's Trail. If you choose this alternative, cross Kinney Road to the trailhead. Prospector's Trail crosses a good-sized, normally dry creekbed, and climbs a small hill. About halfway up the hill on the left is a very unusual saguaro. It is short, only about ten feet tall, and I counted forty arms.

As you climb the hill, you pass a thick patch of teddy bear cholla. At the top of the hill you can see the other side of the basin and the farms of Avra Valley. The trail goes downhill quickly. As you drop down the hill, look for an old jeep road that intersects the trail. Take this road to the right. In a spot or two the road seems to disappear, but keep bearing right and you will soon come to a wide section of the road that leads directly to the Ironwood picnic area, where there are shelters and picnic tables. When you reach the road, walk left to the end of the paved road leading to the rest-rooms. Cross the deep wash to the right. Up the side of the wash is a very distinct trail. Go to the right, heading directly to Golden Gate Mountain. The trail is flat and easy to follow. Vegetation is sparse. It parallels and then crosses a deep wash before turning into an old road. The road comes quickly to a parking area by the paved road. Across Kinney Road is another parking area with a small sign reading Trail. This is the road that loops back to the Golden Gate Trail.

Kinney Road Access Trail

General Description

An easy connecting trail to use for a loop hike with the
David Yetman Trail

Difficulty

Easy

Best time of year to hike

Winter

Length

1.4 miles to intersection with David Yetman Trail

Elevation

2640 feet at trailer park; 2900 feet at Yetman intersection

Miles to trailhead from Speedway/Campbell intersection

11.9

Directions to trailhead from Speedway/Campbell intersection

Go west on Speedway to Interstate 10. Go east on I-10 2.7
miles to the I-19 exit. Exit on I-19 and go 1.3 miles to the
Ajo Way exit. Follow Ajo Way 5.2 miles to Kinney Road.
Turn right on Kinney Road, go 2 miles to Tucson Estates
Parkway. This road is easy to miss. It is .3 miles past the
Western Way intersection. Turn right on Tucson Estates
Parkway. The trailhead is on an unpaved road to the left
and is visible right before you reach the gate of the Foothills
housing development.

This popular trail connects with the David Yetman Trail and is
frequently used by the residents of Tucson Mountain Estates and the
Foothills. A number of combinations can be worked out involving
the David Yetman and Starr Pass trails.

From the parking area a sign indicates Trail Ahead. The trail is
flat and smooth and quickly comes to a sandy wash and bears
slightly to the right. There are a number of paths, and it appears
confusing, but all paths cross the wash and converge on the main
trail. The trails heads directly across the flat desert and then veers
right again, heading directly toward Golden Gate Mountain. The
trail rambles across small drainages, but it is never difficult. On this

Kinney Road Access Trail

lower portion of the trail you can sometimes hear shots from the
Tucson Mountain Park Rifle Range. After about half a mile you can
see two large tanks, which you later learn are water storage tanks
and part of the city of Tucson water system.

Saguaros are scarce in this area, although there are a few
giants and a number of small ones growing in the shelter of the palo
verde trees. Unfortunately, this is not a quiet desert ramble. In
addition to the sound of the rifle range and the automobiles on
Kinney Road, there are the sounds of jets as they approach for
landing at Tucson International Airport and Davis-Monthan Air Force
Base. The trail soon intersects with an old road and follows the road
to the right. The road goes to the water facility. As you near the
tanks, another road leads straight to the parking area for the trailhead, and you can see your car. This is a private road, however,
and you should return to your car via the trail.

Just ahead of the water tanks the trail turns to the right. It is
possible to continue past the water tanks to the left and end up at
the base of the cliffs. This is a difficult trail, but its elevation gain
provides good views of the area. The correct trail is wide, smooth,
and sandy. It meanders across the desert, crossing small drainages.
It is a very pleasant stroll. After .2 miles the trail forks to the right,
but you should continue straight ahead. The general direction of the
trail is to the north, toward the pass between the mountains. The
trail is generally easy to follow. At one point there is a definite fork
and, because it is unsigned, it is confusing. Either fork is all right to
follow, as the two trails converge in a short time. Past this fork the
trail crosses a deeper drainage that could be filled with water after a
rain. After a mile the trail comes to an intersection with an old road.
Mountain bikers have permission to use the trails of the Tucson
Mountains, and this trail is very popular. Two large cairns mark this
spot. Turn to the left, toward the mountains. A short distance and a
gradual elevation gain and you come to a triangular fork in the
road. A sign indicates that this is the David Yetman Trail. From here
the Kinney Road hiker can go right to the Camino de Oeste trailhead or left to the Gates Pass trailhead. It is fun to arrange a three-
car hike, trade car keys along the trail, and meet at a restaurant for
lunch.

Starr Pass Trail

General Description

A short trail through a spectacular low mountain pass that serves as a connecting trail with other trails in the Tucson Mountains

Difficulty

Easy

Best time of year to hike

Winter

Length

.9 miles

Elevation

2700 feet at trailhead; 2790 feet in pass; 2768 feet at intersection

Miles to trailhead from Speedway/Campbell intersection

12.1

Directions to trailhead from Speedway/Campbell intersection

Go west on Speedway to Interstate 10. Go east on I-10 2.7 miles to the I-19 exit. Exit on I-19 and go 1.3 miles to the Ajo Way exit. Follow Ajo Way 5.2 miles to Kinney Road. Turn right on Kinney Road, go .8 miles to Sarasota Boulevard. Turn right on Sarasota and follow the road past the trailer park until it reaches a dead end. Turn right until you see the trailhead.

The Starr Pass Trail is only .9 miles in its entirety. I include it in the trail descriptions because it serves as the connecting point for several trails in the Tucson Mountains. For example, you can park one vehicle at the David Yetman trailheads, another at the Starr Pass trailhead, trade car keys, and avoid duplicating your path. There are a number of combinations that can be worked out.

Aside from its possibilities as a loop trail, Starr Pass goes through some very unusual terrain, through a low pass with Cat Mountain on the right and an unnamed peak on the left.

Originally built in January of 1884 by Richard A. Starr, the route was a quick route from downtown Tucson to the booming

Starr Pass Trail

mine town of Quijotoa, seventy miles southwest of Tucson. It was intended as a toll road, but it is doubtful that this was realized, because the mines played out by 1885. Also, in January of 1884, the Arizona Telegraph Company was incorporated and planned to connect Tucson and Quijotoa by telegraph. The contract was awarded to Starr and J. A. Browder, who completed the line in April of 1884. Today most of the original Starr Pass Road is part of Tucson Mountain Park.

The area is still a significant part of the Tucson scene. An 8,340-foot-long tunnel bores its way to the right of the pass through Cat Mountain to deliver water from the Central Arizona Project treatment facility to the Tucson storage facility near Twenty-second Street. You can see this facility from the David Yetman Trail as it exits on Camino de Oeste. You may wonder why the tunnel was built when the logical plan would be to build the storage facility near the treatment plant. According to Al Stites, chief inspector for the tunnel, it cost less to build the tunnel than to purchase property and utility easements. Even at that, the total cost of the tunnel was $12 million.

As is true with most of the trails in this section of the Tucson Mountains, it is like a maze. Side trails go off in every direction, and it is sometimes hard to know for sure which route you should take. The Starr Pass Trail is no expection. The trail goes through a fence gate and begins gradually to climb. At the top of the first hill, the trail splits. Keep to the left. The trail is sandy and is easy to walk on at first. You pass a wash on the left, and the vegetation is thick. Side trails off to the right are where people climb up Cat Mountain.

The main trail enters a small drainage and stays in it for .2 miles through huge boulders. Many saguaro cling to the sides of the cliff. You pass through the remains of a steel gate. Right past this gate, the trail reaches the top of the rise, and you can see the Catalinas to the north. Continue straight ahead, ignoring any side trails. The trail goes gradually downhill, and this is a very nice section.

As the trail continues downhill, it briefly enters a section that is rocky and hard to walk on. Right past this section you come to a trail intersection. Turn to the left. In a short distance there is another fork. This time do not turn to the left but continue straight ahead. Soon there is another fork. This time keep to the right. The Starr Pass Trail generally follows the route of the utility lines. Very quickly you come to a signed intersection. This is a major intersection and the place where you can meet other hikers for key exchanges.

Brown Mountain Trail Loop

General Description
> *A ridge hike with spectacular views of the Tucson Valley*

Difficulty
> *Moderate, few areas of steep climbing*

Best time of year to hike
> *Winter, early spring, late fall*

Length
> *5 miles*

Elevation
> *2725 feet at trailhead; 3098 feet at high point on trail*

Miles to trailhead from Speedway/Campbell intersection
> *14.5*

Directions to trailhead from Speedway/Campbell intersection
> *Go west on Speedway, through Gates Pass to the intersection with Kinney Road. (Speedway becomes Gates Pass Road at Anklam Road.) Turn right on Kinney Road for 2.3 miles to the Juan Santa Cruz picnic area, which is on the left and before the Arizona-Sonora Desert Museum. The trailhead is .4 miles into the picnic area and is marked with a sign.*

The Brown Mountain Trail Loop is an unusual trek along a ridge in the heart of the Tucson Mountains. Brown Mountain is the first and highest of four peaks on the ridge. The peak was named for Cornelius B. Brown, Pima County agricultural agent from 1920 to 1945, who was instrumental in the creation of Tucson Mountain Park in 1929. Brown is remembered as the Father of Tucson Mountain Park.

Park to the left of the trailhead sign and follow the arrow to the trail. As you can see, many people have made the mistake of scrambling immediately down into the deep drainage beside the parking area. This is not necessary as the correct trail has stair steps down into the drainage, making a much easier beginning to the Brown Mountain Trail Loop.

The trail heads east along the side of Brown Mountain. There is a gradual elevation gain for the first two hundred yards until the trail

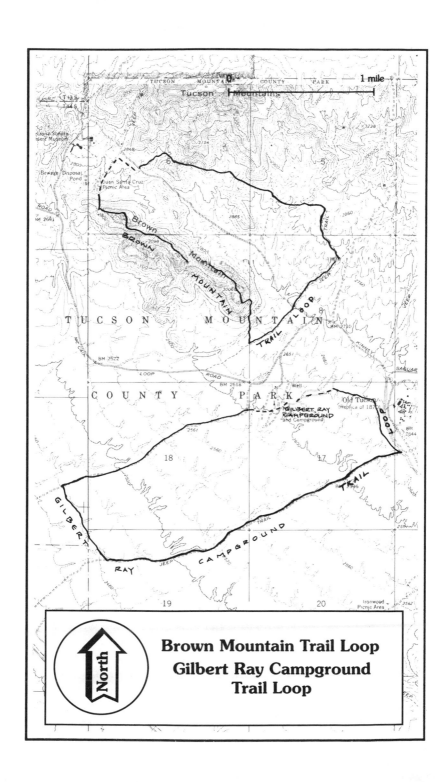

Brown Mountain Trail Loop
Gilbert Ray Campground
Trail Loop

switchbacks to the right and climbs more steeply. To the west are excellent views of the Arizona-Sonora Desert Museum. At the end of a long switchback you come to the top of a ridge and a signed trail intersection. This lookout spot provides great views of the western valley where Baboquivari Peak and Kitt Peak are the dominant landmarks. To the southwest you can trace the canal of the Central Arizona Project. The Brown Mountain Trail follows the sign to the left, pointing to the Gilbert Ray Campground.

The trail continues for a short distance through the deep red iron oxide soil along the west side of the ridge before switchbacking again to the north side of the ridge. There are several paths where hikers have shortcut the trail in their effort to shorten their hike. It is best to stay on the trail, which alternates from one side of the ridge to the other and gains elevation gradually. The trail never works its way to the top of the first peak, which is Brown Mountain. However, it is an easy bushwack to the top if you want to get a sweeping view or watch the sunset.

The trail switchbacks rather steeply down Brown Mountain. It dips into a ravine and gradually climbs the other side of the mountain, at times steep, but nothing that could be termed difficult. The trail rounds the ridge, climbs more steeply, and eventually switchbacks west and climbs to the south side of the ridge. Behind you is an excellent view of Brown Mountain, and you can see the path that is beaten out to the summit. The Arizona-Sonora Desert Museum again stands out, as do the farms of the Avra Valley area.

For the next half mile the trail goes along the top of the ridge. This is an exciting part of the trail, with excellent views in all directions. A short elevation gain brings you to the top of the third peak, and now you can for the first time see Old Tucson Studios, a movie set and tourist attraction. There are good views of Golden Gate Mountain, the backdrop for many western movies.

To the northeast of Old Tucson Studios, Gates Pass winds its way down between the mountains. To the left of Gates Pass and high on the ridge are two houses that look like doll houses from your vantage point. These homes were the scene of an environmental controversy in the late 1970s. They were built by partners in a construction firm who were accused of flagrantly violating the community's wishes by bulldozing a road to the homesite just before the Pima County Board of Supervisors passed an ordinance preventing building on steep slopes and ridges. In 1977 vandals hot-wired

Brown Mountain Trail

a bulldozer and knocked down the walls of the houses, then under construction. The following year both houses were damaged by fires of suspicious origin. The controversy resurfaced late in 1986 when the owner of one of the homes requested permission to double the size of his house, as well as add a guest house and heliport. After much debate, the Pima County Board of Supervisors approved the expansion of the house but denied permission for the guest house and heliport. The owner agreed to stabilize the road and add vegetation to help conceal the road to the houses.

The trail now switchbacks off the high point of this ridge, again through the red iron oxide soil, and drops to a lower ridge. The trail is still a "ridge ramble" and, even though the elevation is not very high, the views remain excellent.

After crossing a short saddle, the trail climbs briefly to a flat area that looks like a saguaro nursery. From one spot I could count twenty small saguaro, not more than two feet tall. This is very unusual because the area is not a protected one normally thought capable of supporting such a heavy growth of young cacti. The trail is lined with boulders, and walking through this area is like walking through a well-manicured English garden.

After the saguaro "garden," the trail circles to the north and drops down the ridge. The Gilbert Ray Campground is visible from here. In winter there are at least one hundred campers in every conceivable type of camping rig enjoying a respite from northern winters. This part of the trail is very rocky and steep as it drops into the valley. Our plan is to cross Kinney Road and loop back to the Juan Santa Cruz picnic area.

As the trail continues down the ridge, it passes through a stand of old weatherbeaten saguaro. At the bottom the trail heads directly away from Kinney Road for .2 miles, and you may wonder if you have made the wrong turn. Don't worry, the trail turns east and drops into a drainage that has a signed trail intersection. A trail leads to the Gilbert Ray Campground from this intersection. To complete the Brown Mountain Trail Loop, make a sharp left and follow the sign to Kinney Road.

In sharp contrast to the switchbacks, the trail is now flat and smooth. It passes through thick vegetation—palo verde, saguaro, barrel cactus. A large drainage is to the right, and the water flowing through here during times of rain no doubt account for the thickness of the growth. Soon the picnic shelters of the Brown Mountain

picnic area come into view. As the trail winds its way to Kinney
Road, it crosses a wash on a man-made walkway. You come
upon a short post with the number sixteen on it, and then one
with the number fifteen. These posts were part of a nature trail
project constructed in the early 1970s by the Youth Conservation
Corps. At post number fifteen the trail forks. Go to the left and you
pass a series of short posts with numbers all the way to one.
Post number one is at Kinney Road. Across the road is a parking
area with a yellow gate. Cross Kinney Road and go through the
gate.

This is a short loop back to the Juan Santa Cruz picnic area
that avoids the switchbacks of returning by the Brown Mountain
Trail. It is not a particularly scenic trail but serves the purpose. The
trail is now wide and flat. It leads to an intersection at the line of
utility poles. Here you turn left and basically follow the utility access
road to the west. Although you are near Kinney Road, the traffic
sounds are blocked by a low ridge. To the left you can see the trail
that goes along the side of Brown Mountain that you just traversed.
The trail climbs gradually, dropping into small drainages occasionally. To the right you can see some evidence of early mining
activity high on a ridge.

For most of the way you can see a steep hill ahead of you that
you will soon climb. This is the hardest part of this trail. It is rather
steep and has loose rocks. As you top out this hill, the road disappears, and there is no sign of a trail; however, you are very close
to the museum and Kinney Road, so it is easy to return to the Juan
Santa Cruz picnic area without a trail.

A hiking adage, "When in doubt follow the utility poles," comes
into play here! (Actually, I'm not sure this is a genuine adage, but it
works in this case.) A steep and rocky path leads downhill. It comes
to a flat area that was at one time a road or a construction area, as
evidenced by several piles of concrete. Cross this flat area and look
to the left. There is an old road that leads to Kinney Road. Because
you can see the cars going by, it is impossible to miss. You quickly
come to a cable across the road and a small sign that reads Road
Closed. Climb over the cable, cross Kinney Road, and .1 miles
ahead is the sign to the Juan Santa Cruz picnic area. Walk facing
traffic to the entrance of the picnic area, and return to your car.
The short jaunt along Kinney Road is the most dangerous part of
this trail!

The map distributed by the Tucson Mountain Parks Department shows this return loop ending up at the King Canyon trailhead and then crossing the Arizona-Sonora Desert Museum and returning to the picnic area. This trail is no longer very well defined, and it is easier to cross in the manner I described. The total time required for the Brown Mountain Trail Loop is approximately two and one-half to three hours. The final section on the north side of Kinney Road takes one-half hour at most.

Gilbert Ray Campground Trail Loop

General Description

A basically flat trail; with many small saguaros thriving under the protection of palo verde trees

Difficulty

Easy

Best time of year to hike

Winter, early spring, late fall

Length

5.3 miles

Elevation

2600 feet at campground; very little elevation loss or gain

Miles to trailhead from Speedway/Campbell intersection

12.5

Directions to trailhead from Speedway/Campbell intersection

Go west on Speedway, over Gates Pass to the intersection with Kinney Road. Turn right on Kinney Road for .7 miles to the Gilbert Ray Campground, which is on the left. The trail begins to the right of camping space A31.

Gilbert Ray was the first director of the Tucson Parks and Recreation Department. From March of 1947 until his retirement in December of 1972, he oversaw the development of the Tucson parks system. Gilbert Ray Campground Trail Loop makes a loop around the campground named in his honor. This trail loop is perfect for someone who wants to see what it is like out in the desert but is not interested in a strenuous hike. It wanders about with a minimum of elevation loss or gain—in fact, the only variation in the trail is in and out of washes.

Drive around the campground, following the signs to space A31. Park so as not to block access should an RV-er want to use the space. To the right of the space is a small sign reading Trail.

This short segment of the trail is for campers who want to walk over to Old Tucson Studios. After less than two hundred yards you come to a deep ravine. The trail dips into the ravine, and there is a hand rail to steady your descent. If you prefer not to use this handrail,

Saguaro thrives under palo verde "nurse" tree, Gilbert Ray Campground Loop Trail

there is a path a few yards to the right that slopes gradually into the wash and connects back with the main trail.

The trail is actually an old road that quickly comes to an intersection. Across the road is Old Tucson Studios. You want to go to the right and follow the route of the utility line across the desert. The trail is now heading southwest and is basically a utility access road at this point. Probably because it is for the most part a flat trail and easy to reach, the Gilbert Ray Campground Trail Loop is popular with horseback riders and mountain bikers, both permitted on the trails of Tucson Mountain Park.

There are mostly old saguaros along the first part of the route. Vegetation increases in drainages where mesquite and palo verde thrive. Creosote bushes grow in abundance, as do prickly pear, cholla, and barrel cacti. If you are on the trail in the early morning or late afternoon, you may see some javelina. Their footprints are everywhere, especially in the drainages.

Along one particularly large drainage, water has cut deep banks. Although the heat would be uncomfortable, it would be interesting to hike this trail after a summer storm. As the trail progresses, it gets farther away from civilization and, for a short time, the only signs of man are the utility poles.

This absence of civilization does not last, and after about half a mile, you spot a trailer, a stable, and some horses. When you see the trailer, begin looking carefully for a turnoff to the right, which may be marked by a cairn. The trail turns immediately to the right, crosses a wash, and is no longer a road but a narrow trail. If you made the correct turn, you should be going away from the utility poles and the trailer.

The interesting part of this section of the trail is the number of small saguaro thriving under the palo verde trees. The palo verde trees "nurse," or shelter, the saguaro until it is strong enough to thrive on its own. One palo verde tree in this section shelters thirteen small saguaros. It would be interesting to see how these thirteen saguaros fare in years to come, but they grow at the rate of one inch a year, and it is unlikely that any of us will be hiking this way one hundred years from now. In 2090, if all thirteen survive, the palo verde will probably have been choked out of existence, and the saguaros will be a massive tangle of arms!

After half a mile the trail intersects with a road. Turn right on the road to return to the campground. The road is a utility access road and is rarely used. This is a very pleasant walk, mostly flat. There is only one portion where it dips in and out of a small drainage. There are still many palo verde trees with tiny saguaro underneath. This area must be very beautiful in early May when the palo verde trees are covered with tiny yellow blossoms.

As the road curves to the left or north, you can see the Gilbert Ray Campground, and you know that you should be heading off to the right. Keep looking carefully for a side road that leads to the campground. There is usually a cairn as a marker. Also, there are two small saguaros in the middle of the trail. Take this road to the right. It drops almost immediately into a deep ravine. On the right is a pipeline crossing the wash, and there are several underground cable warning posts. As you come out of the ravine you can see picnic shelters, volleyball net poles, and a paved road.

You are back to the Gilbert Ray Campground and picnic area. Turn left on the road toward the park headquarters, marked by the flags flying on a pole. Right before the gate look to the right and you can see direction signs leading to the camp spots. Remember, you are looking for A31. Cross the desert and follow the signs to the camp spot. It doesn't take long to get to A31, and it is interesting to see the types of recreational vehicle equipment that people bring to the desert.

When you pass a sign that divides the A section from the B section, a path cuts past the restrooms. This path will lead you directly to parking space A31.

This Gilbert Ray Campground Trail Loop takes two and one-half to three hours and is a good introduction to the desert.

The Rincon Mountains

Rincon means "corner" in Spanish. It is not known for certain how the mountain range to the east of Tucson got its name. Topped by the 8,666-foot Mica Mountain, the Rincons have historically been the least accessible of the four ranges around Tucson.

Hohokam Indians camped and lived in the Rincons as in the Santa Catalina and the Tucson mountains. In Box Canyon five bedrock mortars show where Indian women ground legumes. Petroglyphs adorn rocks and cliffs.

When the Hohokam left, the mountains were generally free of human habitation until the early 1800s, when the Apache wandered in the range. The mining that led to the development of the other ranges was almost nonexistent in the Rincons.

By the late 1800s, the lower areas of the Rincons saw extensive ranching. The main building of the Tanque Verde Guest Ranch today was once the ranch of Emilio Carrillo. Carrillo homesteaded the area in 1877, naming his ranch La Cebadilla for the wild barley that grew in profusion. Carrillo built the solid ranch house with small holes for rifles in case of Indian attack. Rumors persisted that Carrillo kept large sums of money hidden on the ranch. In 1904 a gang of bandits attacked La Cebadilla and demanded money. When Carrillo said he had no money, the robbers hung him from the rafters three times, lowering him each time long enough to ask where the money was hidden. Frightened by an arriving buggy, the bandits fled, leaving Carrillo alive but near death.

Carrillo and other ranchers ran so many cattle in the foothills of the Rincons that vegetation was destroyed for generations to come. Lime kilns, operating in the 1880s, also seriously deforested the area. The remains of these kilns can be seen along the Cactus Forest Trail.

The foothills of the Rincons drew the attention of world-renowned ecologist and University of Arizona president Homer Shantz in the late 1920s. Shantz dreamed of preserving the magnificent stand of saguaros for use as a study area. Through his efforts the state did purchase the land, but when the depression hit, the state was unable to keep up the payments. Through a property transfer agreement, the federal government took over in 1933, establishing the Saguaro National Monument. Additional property was purchased from private individuals in the early 1970s. Today the monument is managed by the National Park Service.

In 1939, a few years after the establishment of the monument, great numbers of the giant saguaro began to rot and die. Coincidentally, in February of that year, the coldest temperatures ever recorded caused the mercury to fall to twenty-five degrees and remain there for several hours. At first plant scientists did not make any connection between the low temperature and the diseased plants. By 1941 so many saguaro were dying that the National Park Service removed diseased arms and buried whole plants that showed evidence of the rot. Plans were considered for transplanting young saguaro in the area. Before this was implemented, the policy of the National Park Service became more accepting of nature and did not interfere with the natural progression of plant life.

In the two decades that followed, extensive studies were conducted on the saguaro population. The studies led scientists to conclude that the freeze of 1939 had weakened the old giant saguaro by making them susceptible to the bacterial infection, and that the demise of the saguaro was part of the natural cycle in its long life. Younger, stronger plants are able to fight off infection by forming a "boot" or callus and sealing off the disease from the rest of the plant.

The Rincons were as cool and attractive as the Santa Catalinas, but few took advantage of their heights. One who did was Levi Manning, a mayor of Tucson and former surveyor general of the United States. He discovered a flat area at about eight thousand feet near Mica Mountain and decided to homestead the area. In preparation for this, he had Mexican laborers build a wagon road to the site. A well-constructed log cabin was built, and for a few years Manning Camp was the social center of Tucson in the summer. He even hauled a piano to the site. However, his homestead application had not been approved when the Rincon Mountains became part of the Coronado National Forest, and it was declared void. Manning abandoned the camp and never returned.

The United States Forest Service began using the cabin and the site in the early 1920s to set up a permanent fire control center. The camp was spruced up with modern conveniences and additional bunkhouses over the years, eventually including a television set. The cost of maintaining the camp became too expensive, and in 1976 everything was dismantled but the original log cabin that Manning built in the early 1900s. That cabin is used by the staff of the Saguaro National Monument when working in the area.

In the mid-1950s, the Park Service drew up plans to develop the Rincon Mountains in a manner similar to the Mount Lemmon area. A nineteen-mile road called the Desert Mountain Highway would be constructed from the monument headquarters to Manning Camp. The thinking at the time was that such development would relieve the stress on the Mount Lemmon area, and that the rapid growth of the Tucson area demanded more recreational facilities. Fortunately for hikers who enjoy the wilderness, the Desert Mountain Highway never materialized.

Today, reaching the highlands of the Rincons requires backpacking. Unlike the trails in the Santa Catalinas, which steeply and quickly ascend into the high country, many miles of foothills must be covered before reaching the ponderosa pine level.

Because this guide is restricted to hikes that can be completed in one day, I have only included five hikes in the Rincon Mountains. One is an exceptionally easy trek along the Cactus Forest Trail. A second easy hike climbs Pink Hill and goes to Little Wild Horse Tank. The Douglas Spring and Tanque Verde Ridge trails are long but relatively easy hikes across the foothills to about the six thousand-foot level. The area around Douglas Spring was burned in the summer of 1989 in the Chiva fire. The only hike I have included that gets you into the high country is the hike to Rincon Peak.

Cactus Forest Trail

General Description
A basically flat ramble across the desert, through many
varieties of cacti and some old lime kilns
Difficulty
Easy
Best time of year to hike
Winter, late fall, early spring
Length
5.2 miles one way
Elevation
2760 feet at the trailhead; 2960 feet at Old Spanish Trail
Miles to trailhead from Speedway/Campbell intersection
13.9
Directions to trailhead from Speedway/Campbell intersection
Go south on Campbell to the intersection with Broadway.
Turn east (left) on Broadway, following it until 1500 yards
before it reaches a dead end. A large sign on the right
marks the beginning of the Cactus Forest Trail

The Cactus Forest Trail meanders across the desert from Broadway Boulevard to Old Spanish Trail and is a good introduction to the lowlands of the Rincon Mountains. The ideal way to hike this trail is to leave a vehicle at the trailhead parking area on Old Spanish Trail and begin the hike from the Broadway trailhead.

A large sign and a map of the Cactus Forest Trail system marks the beginning of the trail. The trail begins to the left of the map, and each intersection is well marked. After .1 miles a sign indicates the beginning of the Shantz Trail. The Cactus Forest Trail follows the arrow to the right.

The smooth, sandy trail passes many old, giant saguaro. Although palo verde and mesquite trees "nurse" a number of young saguaro, this area is primarily an aging saguaro forest. The saguaro and an abundance of other cactus varieties make the name Cactus Forest Trail appropriate.

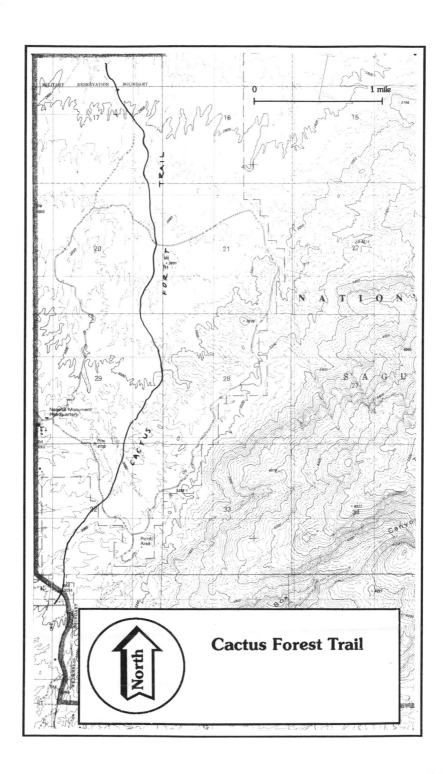

Cactus Forest Trail

Lime kilns first used in 1880s, Cactus Forest Trail

For most of the trail there is little elevation gain or loss. Mostly level, the trail drops in and out of several small drainages and occasionally crosses a sandy wash. At .7 miles a sign indicates the intersection with the Cholla Trail. To stay on the Cactus Forest Trail, continue straight ahead. This section has many creosote bushes. Rub a few leaves and smell your fingers, and you will realize why it is called creosote, although the plant has nothing to do with the actual substance. In early spring the tiny yellow flowers of the creosote bush make a showy display.

At .3 miles past the Cholla Trail intersection, another sign marks a side trail to the Mica View picnic area. Again, continue straight ahead, following the arrow to the Mesquite Trail. At the Mesquite Trail intersection, continue straight ahead. As you can see, the trail is indeed well marked. One reason for this is that horseback riding is permitted on these trails, and many side trails have been made by riders seeking shortcuts.

As you approach the paved road of Saguaro National Monument East, you see a small hill to the left called Observatory Hill. When this area was owned by the University of Arizona there was some discussion about building an observatory on this hill, and the top was leveled, but the property was acquired by the federal government before any such plans materialized. By the drive is a sign for the Cactus Forest trailhead, at which point you will have come 1.8 miles. Cross the road in the painted crosswalk, and continue the trail on the other side. In a few hundred yards you pass some concrete foundations on the right. This was the location of the first ranger station in the monument.

Nine-tenths of a mile from Cactus Forest Drive are the lime kilns, large beehive structures to the left and below the trail. A sign explains that these kilns were constructed around 1880. Limestone was brought down from the nearby hills and heated to a very high temperature to form lime. The lime was used in producing mortar and whitewash. Each batch of lime burned about twelve cords of wood from nearby trees. Carmen Moreno operated the kilns from 1914 to 1917, selling lime to Tucson building contractors for ten dollars a ton. This lime was used in the construction of the rock wall around the University of Arizona. In 1920 ranchers forced the closure of the kilns because of the destruction of cattle forage. A warning that bee colonies now inhabit the kilns is not needed, as the bees prohibit close inspection of the kilns. Also, as I leaned over to attempt to take a picture of one of the kilns, a huge rattler encouraged me on my way! The kilns are an important part of the history of this area and should be left undisturbed.

Past the lime kilns, the Cactus Forest Trail goes through an area with very few cacti. Short grasses and a type of low, gray-green shrub predominate. Here the trail begins to climb slightly for the first time, going up and down a series of small hills, making a nice change. The sweeping views of the surrounding mountain ranges are dramatic.

As the trail nears West Cactus Forest Drive, there are many side trails that can be confusing, again due to the large number of horseback riders in the area. Continue straight ahead. The trail is wide and sandy at this point. To the left is a large wash that has cut quite a swath in times of heavy runoff. There are many large mesquite trees. It is in this area that great horned owls breed. The trail becomes an old road in this area, and again there are very few cacti, just a few prickly pears and chollas.

The trail crosses West Cactus Forest Drive and continues .9 miles to Old Spanish Trail. Hopefully you will have left a vehicle in the parking area. Otherwise, it's 5.2 miles back to the Broadway trailhead.

Pink Hill–Wentworth Trail Loop

General Description
A hike to a small pool past a dam built by an early rancher, and across an old airstrip

Difficulty
Moderate, some areas of steep switchbacks

Best time of year to hike
Winter, early spring, late fall

Length
8 miles Pink Hill-Wentworth Loop

Elevation
2760 feet at the trailhead; 3240 feet at Little Wild Horse Tank

Miles to trailhead from Speedway/Campbell intersection
13.9

Directions to trailhead from Speedway/Campbell intersection
Go south on Campbell to the intersection with Broadway Boulevard. Turn east (left) on Broadway and follow it until a sign indicates it is 1500 yards before it dead-ends. The Pink Hill Trail begins at the Cactus Forest trailhead on the right of Broadway.

Wild Horse Canyon is a rugged and beautiful canyon that can be reached by using a combination of the Shantz, Pink Hill, Squeeze Pen, Carrillo and Wild Horse trails. Pink Hill is a small cone-shaped hill 1.6 miles from the trailhead. So named because the iron oxide content of the soil makes it pink, the hill is barely noticeable from the desert floor. However, as you ascend the trail and are able to look down on the hill, it stands out as a definite "pink" hill. After reaching Wild Horse Canyon, we will return to the trailhead via the Wild Horse, Wentworth and Loma Verde trails.

As you must realize by the number of trails already mentioned, you work your way through a maze enroute to Wild Horse Canyon. The trails, which were created by the many horseback riders who frequent the area, have been made less confusing by new signs recently installed by the Park Service, administrators of the Saguaro National Monument, Rincon Unit. Unfortunately, the signs themselves

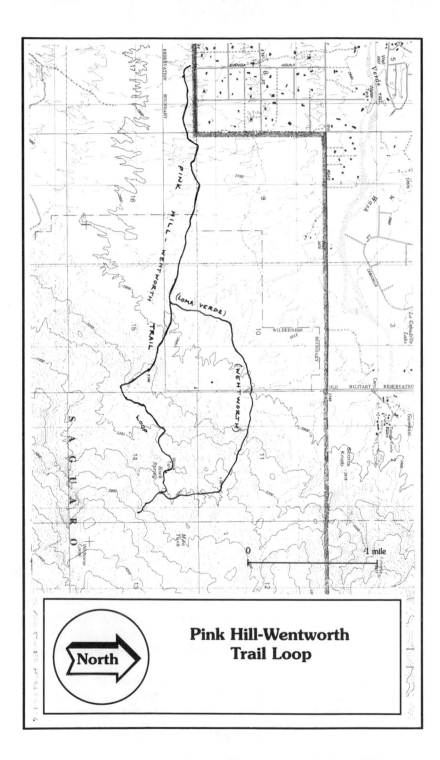

**Pink Hill-Wentworth
Trail Loop**

Little Wild Horse Tank, Pink Hill-Wentworth Trail Loop before heavy runoff after the Chiva fire filled most of the pond

are a bit confusing. The trail you are currently on is written at the top of the sign in capital letters and has no directional arrow. Trails that cut off the main trail are indicated in smaller letters with a directional arrow indicating the direction to turn. The following instructions are quite specific.

Begin at the Cactus Forest trailhead. Go left on the Shantz Trail, following the arrow pointing to the Pink Hill Trail. At the Pink Hill intersection turn to the right, towards the mountains. The trail crosses several small washes before coming to a deeper, more pronounced wash. A trail intersection sign marks the meeting of the Loma Verde and Pink Hill trails. Remember it, as this is where you will rejoin the Pink Hill Trail on your return. The Pink Hill Trail continues straight ahead. It is a rocky, fairly steep, short climb to the top.

This is a favorite spot for horseback riders and the top is practically barren of vegetation. There are excellent views from this spot, particularly of the Catalina and Tucson mountains and most of the city of Tucson. As you look toward the Rincons, you can see Wild Horse Canyon and the trail climbing the side of the mountain into the canyon. Garwood Dam, a large concrete structure near the base of the drainage of Wild Horse Canyon, is barely visible. The Saguaro Trail goes to the left off Pink Hill. Your goal is to continue toward the mountains, descending the hill to the intersection of the Squeeze Pen Trail.

Turn right on the Squeeze Pen Trail. For .2 miles you will head south, away from the Rincons. When you reach the Carrillo Trail intersection, turn left, and you are again heading toward the mountains. Many well-marked side trails lead to the left. The correct route is to remain on the Carrillo Trail. The trail goes along the side of and then across a large drainage, which is the drainage out of Wild Horse Canyon. Most of the year there is some water in the wash. The vegetation is lush. Reeds grow in the pools and in early spring there are wildflowers everywhere.

As you cross the wash a side trail leads to the right. Ignore it and follow the trail that bears left and makes a short climb out of the drainage. From this part of the trail there are excellent views of the dam. It is slightly to the right and across the base of the drainage. This dam was built in the 1920s by a rancher named Garwood as a water supply. A small room at the base of the dam was used as a cool room for storage of food.

Enroute to the dam you will pass the cutoff for the Deer Valley, Kennedy and Freight Wagon trails. When you reach the turnoff for the Garwood Trail, turn right on the old wagon road that leads to Garwood Dam. This is still the Carrillo Trail. From the road the views of the Tucson Basin are excellent. To the right look carefully and you will be able to pick out the old airstrip that you will be following later. Below you see large pools of water and most of the year there is some water flowing. When you reach the dam you will be surprised at the size of the structure. It is tempting, but unsafe, to walk across the dam.

Past the dam, the trail climbs to the left. This portion of the trail has the steepest elevation gain but is short and near Little Wild Horse Tank. Several unmarked side trails turn right to vantage points on top of the knolls. Keep bearing left until the intersection of the Wild Horse Trail. At the intersection, turn right, through two fence posts, into Wild Horse Canyon. Most of the year the stream is flowing and will require wading or boulder-hopping to cross.

Across the canyon the correct route is to the left and up the

hill. This is a short steep climb that drops quickly to Little Wild
Horse Tank. This area is the destination for many trail rides from
the Tanque Verde Guest Ranch. A small pool provides a permanent
source of water for wildlife. If you care to bushwhack farther up the
canyon there are other pools. This is truly a wild canyon, one
undoubtedly inhabited at one time by wild horses.

To return, retrace your steps across the drainage going through
the fence posts. This time, continue straight on the Wild Horse Trail.
Wild Horse Trail drops into a large drainage in an area where there
are a number of small saguaro. At the intersection of Three Tank
Trail, the Wild Horse Trail begins the descent out of the foothills.
The view of the Tucson valley again spreads out in front. The airstrip is now very distinct. To the left of the trail is a deep chasm cut
by the force of water. Deep, dark pools have led to this section
being called the "Black Hole." Past the pools, the trail drops rather
steeply before flattening out into a smooth easy trail.

When you reach the desert floor, watch for signs indicating the
Wentworth Trail. This is a major intersection with three signs and
can be confusing. The correct route is through the two large fence
posts and to the right and directly north toward the Catalinas. The
sign will indicate "Wentworth Trail—W." After .2 mile, the trail again
turns left and begins to follow the airstrip.

Notice that there are no saguaros for the length of the strip but
there are large saguaros on either side. There was a time when bulldozing saguaro out of the way was an acceptable practice. As you
hike, look back. You can clearly see that this was once a landing
strip. I have devoted considerable time to finding out who built this
landing strip, but have so far been unsuccessful. Perhaps it was a
secret airstrip for weapons testing in World War II or a rancher's
private plane landing strip or a rum runner's rendezvous point
or . . . ?

As the trail leaves the airstrip, it continues along the side of a
wide wash for a short distance, then turns left and starts across the
wash. In the wash a sign indicates that the Wentworth Trail continues right along the bottom of the drainage. There will be an old
fence line on your right. You cross a wide, sandy wash, and then
go through a grassy bottom, under spreading mesquite and along a
fence line. This section is unlike the rest of the hike. This is an area
where cattle would love to graze and, in an earlier day, did.

After about .3 miles of this grassy mesquite area you come to a trail intersection. This is the Loma Verde Trail. Continue left .6 miles until the intersection of the Pink Hill Trail. Turn right on the Pink Hill Trail. When you reach the intersection of the Shantz Trail, bear left and in .3 miles you will see the signs of the Cactus Forest trailhead. The entire loop will take about four hours.

Tanque Verde Ridge Trail

General Description

> A long hike, mostly along the ridge line through changing
> vegetation to the Juniper Basin Campground

Difficulty

> Moderate, some areas of steep climbing

Best time of year to hike

> Winter, early spring, late fall

Length

> 6.9 miles to Juniper Basin

Elevation

> 3100 feet at the trailhead; 6000 feet at Juniper Basin
> Campground

Miles to trailhead from Speedway/Campbell intersection

> 11.5 to Visitor Center parking lot; 1 to Javelina picnic area

Directions to trailhead from Speedway/Campbell intersection

> Go south on Campbell to the intersection with Broadway
> Boulevard. Turn east (left) on Broadway and follow until
> the intersection with Old Spanish Trail. Turn right on Old
> Spanish Trail to the entrance of Saguaro National Monu-
> ment East. Enter the monument (there is a $3 fee) and
> follow signs to the Javelina Picnic Area. A sign indicates the
> parking area for the Tanque Verde Ridge Trail.

Tanque verde, Spanish for "green tank," is a name often used
in the Rincon Mountains. There's a Tanque Verde wash, falls,
canyon, ridge, peak, guest ranch, and, of course, hiking trail. In the
1860s rancher William Oury tried to avoid Indian attacks on his
cattle by moving the entire herd to the base of a ridge on the southeast corner of the Rincons. Two large water holes (or tanks) contain-
ing green algae were on the range, and the area came to be
referred to as Tanque Verde.

The Tanque Verde Trail follows Tanque Verde Ridge to Juniper Basin
and on to Cowhead Saddle. There it connects with the Cowhead Saddle
Trail to continue the climb to Manning Camp. The section of the trail
that ends at Juniper Basin makes an excellent, although long, day hike.

71

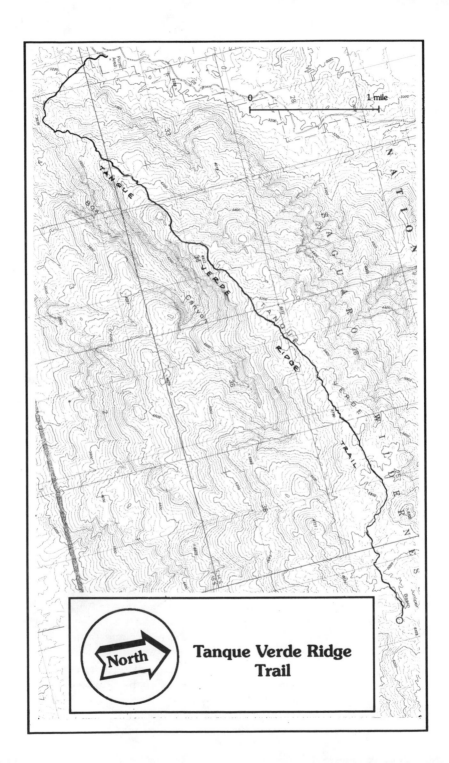

Tanque Verde Ridge Trail

Juniper Basin Campground, elevation 6000 feet; Tanque Verde Ridge Trail

The trail begins to the right of the Javelina Picnic Area. It goes slightly downhill and crosses a small drainage before beginning to climb. There are many cacti in this area, including several large, healthy saguaro. Past another small drainage is a trail register.

After the trail register, the climb is steeper, and you quickly come to a good lookout point from which you can see the telescopes on Kitt Peak and most of the southern part of Tucson. After this lookout point, the trail levels out and is smooth and sandy for a short distance before dropping into another drainage. As the trail climbs out of this drainage, the climb increases and the views get better. You can see all of Tucson, and on a clear day you can see as far north as Picacho Peak. Occasionally there is a faint side trail where hikers have gone for a better view, but the correct route is always easy to follow.

The first part of the trail follows a pattern of crossing small drainages and leveling out for some distance, with the views of the valley ever improving. After about one and one-half miles you top out on the ridge, and you can see why the name Tanque Verde Ridge Trail is justified. Most of the trail from here on follows the ridge line, going to either the north or south, but always coming back to the ridge. The views from the ridge are spectacular. To the south in the Santa Ritas are Mount Wrightson and Mount Hopkins. Ahead and to the southeast is Rincon Peak. To the west are the Tucson Mountains, and to the north, a magnificent view of the Santa Catalinas.

The vegetation is typical of this elevation. Saguaro, prickly pear, cholla, ocotillo, and hedgehog make this area especially pretty when the cacti bloom in mid-April. As you leave the ridge line and begin to circle the hill to the north, there is a deep drainage on the left. Along this section of the trail is a small sign that indicates that you have reached the four thousand-foot elevation level. Past the sign is a drainage that occasionally holds small pools of water, especially after a summer rain. There are long stretches of flat, easy walking, with only slight elevation gain. Rarely do you find a shady spot. The views continue to be great, and this would be a great place to hike to see the sunset and the lights of the city.

Past the four thousand-foot sign the saguaro become scarce. A few scrub oak begin to appear. There is a large section covered with bear grass. Bear grass is used today by Tohono O'odham basketmakers. Many years ago the sharp-edged grass was used by the Apaches to cut off the nose of any woman accused of adultery.

An interesting feature of this hike is the opportunity to observe the changing vegetation that accompanies the increasing elevation. Past the section covered with bear grass, the first juniper and piñon pine begin to appear. The trail occasionally tops out on the ridge, levels out for a distance, and then drops to the north or south side of the ridge. The views are amazing. This is one of the best parts of this trail with views in all directions.

About three miles past the four thousand-foot marker, you come to another sign that indicates five thousand-foot elevation. By now there are no saguaro. The vegetation is mainly scrub oak, juniper and piñon pine, and manzanita. Past the five thousand-foot elevation sign, shindaggers (amole) begin to appear. You are now far back into the foothills of the Rincons, and the rest of the trail goes up and down small hills. As you progress into the foothills, the trees increase in density and size. The climbs up and down the hills are not too difficult. As you continue along the trail, the city disappears and the views are not as spectacular. You have the feeling of real isolation in this area. The trees appear to be stressed for lack of water, and there are a number of dead manzanita. Rainfall has been below normal for several years.

After you drop into a narrow, sandy stream bed, you are about one mile from the Juniper Basin Campground. For a few hundred yards, there is a section of loose rock that makes the climb more difficult. Red metal strips are on the trees to mark the trail so that it can be followed in the snow.

Soon the trail crosses a wide, flat, rocky area. Several large cairns mark the correct route. Across the rocks the trail goes along the side of a drainage and is a pretty area. The trees are much larger now. You then cross a definite stream bed, with a dark grey rock bottom. There are pretty flowers along the stream, so water must flow in this stream frequently. A few hundred yards past this stream bed is the Juniper Basin Campground.

This is a beautiful area. Reservations must be made at monument headquarters for overnight camping. There are picnic tables, grills, and a toilet. The area is covered with exceptionally large junipers, the bark of which looks much like the skin of an alligator, giving the tree the common name "alligator juniper." The elevation at the campground is six thousand feet. Hiking time is four to five hours, with almost the same time required to return. The Tanque Verde Ridge Trail is a long day hike but not particularly strenuous.

Douglas Spring Trail

General Description
> An interesting hike through an area damaged by a major fire

Difficulty
> Moderate

Best time of year to hike
> Winter, early spring, late fall

Length
> 5.9 miles to Douglas Spring Campground

Elevation
> 2749 feet at the trailhead; 4800 feet at campground

Miles to trailhead from Speedway/Campbell intersection
> 15

Directions to trailhead from Speedway/Campbell intersection
> Go east on Speedway until it reaches a dead end. The trailhead is to the east of the parking area.

The Douglas Spring Trail crosses the foothills of the Rincon Mountains to the Douglas Spring Campground. Past the campground the trail continues to Cowhead Saddle and serves as a connecting trail for several loops used by backpackers. Much of the vegetation on the last six miles of the trail was consumed by the Chiva fire in the summer of 1989. The trail is interesting in that it provides a close-up example of the effects of a major fire.

A lightning strike on 5 July 1989 started a fire near the northern boundary of the Saguaro National Monument. Before it was controlled on 10 July, the fire burned 9,580 acres, including the entire Douglas Spring Campground and much of the Douglas Spring Trail. After being closed for revegetation and rehabilitation for nearly ten months, the trail was reopened in April of 1990. Any off-trail use in this area is still prohibited, as are open campfires at the Douglas Spring Campground.

A sign at the trailhead describes the Manning Camp Trail System. This description will include that portion of the trail to Douglas Spring Campground. The first mile of the trail is flat and

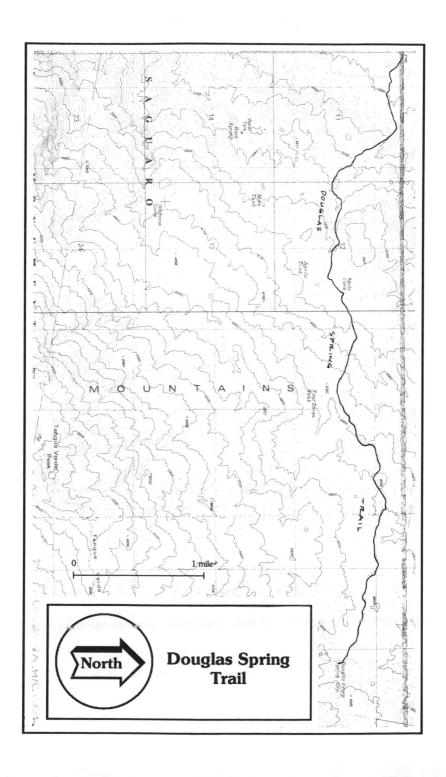

Douglas Spring Trail

Burned out area after Chiva fire—summer of 1989; Douglas Spring Trail

sandy and untouched by the fire. The vegetaton is typical of this elevation—saguaro, prickly pear, barrel, and cholla cacti; ocotillos; palo verde and mesquite trees. After one-quarter of a mile there is a trail register. As you can see by the number of signatures, this is a popular trail.

This first section of the trail goes in and out of small drainages that only have water during rainfall. You will notice that there are very few small saguaros. Before becoming a preserved area, this section was heavily used by ranchers and many small saguaros were trampled by cattle.

After a mile the trail begins to climb gradually, and as you ascend you can see the pink buildings of the Tanque Verde Guest Ranch to the northeast and most of the Tucson Valley. As you ascend the first small hill, the Catalina and Tucson mountains are visible.

The trail goes to the left of the hill and begins to climb more steeply. To the left of the trail is a deep, rugged drainage. Most of the year there are pools of water and some water trickling over the rocks, making this an excellent spot to see wildlife, especially mule deer. As the trail climbs steeply around the hill, you will note that recent trail work has made the trail easy to climb. Steps have been dug into the steep parts, with rocks placed as erosion control. As you top the first hill, you come to a flat spot that is used frequently as a rest stop. You can see a trail beaten out to the top of the hill by hikers who want to see the view. There is no rush to do this as there are several good viewing spots farther along the trail.

From here on the Douglas Spring Trail follows this pattern— climbing or going around the side of the hills, leveling out, even descending briefly, and then climbing again. Occasionally there are faint side trails, but it is always easy to distinguish the main trail.

From the flat spot the trail again begins to climb up the side of another hill, and by now the views of the city are excellent. Again there are good views of the drainage on the left. The trail climbs and switchbacks up the hill, flattens out for a short distance, and then begins climbing again, this time along the right side of the hill. As you round this third hill, you can begin to see some of the damage caused by the Chiva fire. This area is on the outskirts of the main fire damage, and there are spots of green interspersed with burned areas. Most of the vegetation in the drainages was protected from the fire. As you walk along the side of the hill, there is another drainage to the right. This frequently contains water and is also a good spot to see wildlife. As I hiked this trail in early May, I saw seven deer in this section. The trail climbs steeply for a short distance and then once again levels out, continuing to follow the drainage.

From this point on, the fire damage is extensive. The saguaros are brown, but some have a few blossoms on top. The trail crosses several small drainages but continues to follow to the left of the main drainage for a quarter of a mile before turning away and climbing gradually another small hill and then traversing a long flat area. In this flat area you have good views of the inner foothills. Large drainages come down. There are patches of green, but for the most part the vegetation was destroyed by the fire. About half way across this flat area a faint trail intersects. It is used by riders from the Tanque Verde Guest Ranch, and an interesting side hike is to make this a loop, but for now we are continuing straight ahead on the Douglas Spring Trail.

There are several small drainages before crossing a wide, sandy drainage that comes down from a steep, rocky section known as Bridal Wreath Falls. Oddly, in the low basin below the falls there are several acres of lush green mesquite that were totally missed by the fire. A side trail leads off to the right if you would like to take time to explore this green area.

Past this basin the trail begins to climb again, this time quite steeply. The views of the city are impressive. From here to the campground the fire damage is extensive. Fortunately, this is above the level of the saguaro. Most of the area is covered with the black stalks of the ocotillo. The prickly pears are blackened heaps. Occasionally there will be a tree that escaped.

As you climb this hill, you will come to a place where one trail leads off to the left and another goes straight ahead, around and above the drainage that held the falls. Either way is correct. The trail to the left is very steep, probably shorter in distance, but longer in actual hiking. I prefer to continue ahead, above the drainage. This is mostly level or easy climbing. The vegetation in the drainage was protected from the fire, and in spring and fall there are lovely wildflowers. The trail rounds a knoll and continues to follow the drainage, by now a wide, sandy creek. Here the trail is wide and smooth. In the drainage is what remains of a man-made well. After a short distance, the trail goes to the left, away from the drainage.

As you look to the southeast, you can see where the fire swept across the ridges, burning everything in its path. You then come to the intersection with the trail that came straight up the mountain. Turn right, toward the mountains. If you wish, you can take this trail on your return. Now you are on an open knoll, and the city again spreads out below.

As you continue to climb, the higher elevations of the Rincons stand out. The large outcropping of rocks straight ahead is Helen's Dome. A little farther east is Spud Rock, so named because a man of German descent retired from the railroad in about 1890, moved into the Rincon Mountains, and raised potatoes near the rock. To the left and far below you can see a large pond of water. From this point the views of the Catalinas and the city are excellent.

After leaving the side of the hill, the trail rounds the hill, and you now begin a gradual decline into the Douglas Spring Campground, crossing in and out of several drainages, going up and down small hills, until reaching the campground. It is in this area that the fire was most intense.

On my last hike here, mesquite, scrub oak, and juniper pine flourished. Manzanita grew in profusion. It was cool and green. We were celebrating a birthday and hung balloons and streamers in the trees, even climbing a tree to see when the birthday guest was arriving! Now it is all gone. Only the stumps of trees are left. In the midst of the desolation, bright purple verbena spreads a carpet across the gray ash of the fire. In time it will all return. In fact, even now the alligator junipers that appear dead are resprouting.

The campground has been rebuilt. A public restroom, a hitching post, and several signs indicating camp sites make up the Douglas Spring Campground now. Before the fire the trees provided shade, and picnic tables were at each site.

We now know that there are good things about a fire. The deadwood is burned, and new plants have a chance to grow. It is a shock, nevertheless, to hike into an area that was once green and pleasant.

Rincon Peak Trail

General Description
> One of the most beautiful and difficult trails in the Rincon
> Mountains

Difficulty
> Extremely difficult

Best time of year to hike
> Late spring, early fall, summer

Length
> 8.1 miles via Miller Creek Trail

Elevation
> 4250 feet at Miller Creek trailhead; 8482 feet on Rincon Peak

Miles to trailhead from Speedway/Campbell intersection
> 58.9

Directions to trailhead from Speedway/Campbell intersection
> Go west on Speedway to I-10. Follow I-10 east to the
> Mescal exit. Turn left on Mescal Road for 16 miles. Mescal
> Road becomes Forest Service Road 35. At the intersection
> of FS 35 and FS 4407, a sign indicates that the Miller
> Creek trailhead is to the left. The trailhead is .2 miles from
> the sign. Mescal Road and the Forest Service roads are
> unpaved but are suitable for passenger cars.

Rincon Peak, at 8482 feet, is the third highest peak in the
Rincons. The Miller Creek Trail, in combination with the Heartbreak
Ridge and Rincon Peak trails, is the shortest route to the summit.
Although included in this guide as a day hike, one must be an
exceptionally strong hiker to conquer this mountain in one day. If
you plan to do so, it is recommended that you drive to the trailhead
the night before and begin your hike at daybreak.

The trail begins through a gate in the fence that is hard to open and
close. Markers indicate that this is part of the Arizona Trail System.

The first part of the trail is basically level, crossing and recrossing Miller Creek several times. Most of the year there will be water
in the stream, and the resultant vegetation makes for a pretty area.
The sandy and smooth trail passes through manzanitas and under
large Arizona sycamores and Emory oaks. There are a few large
barrel cacti that look out of place in this vegetation.

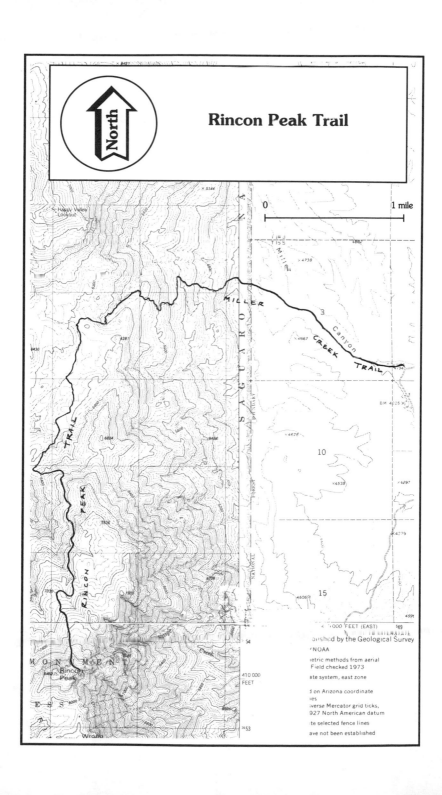

Rincon Peak Trail

*Hiker signing register on summit beside area's largest cairn,
Rincon Peak Trail*

After about three-quarters of a mile you come to a large pool
and a jumble of rocks. Here you cross Miller Creek and then go to
the left of a small drainage. The trail then begins to climb gradually,
leaving the drainage and veering to the right, climbing more steeply for
two hundred yards before dropping into and crossing another drainage.

Immediately across this drainage is a fence and signs marking
the boundary of the Saguaro National Monument. There is a walk-
through opening in the fence. The trail, sandy and rocky, goes
through a thick stand of manzanita, then goes down and crosses a
big boulder-strewn drainage. Across the drainage the trail climbs
steeply. Although there will be some pleasant, level stretches, the
easy part of this trail is over. There are places where the trail splits,
but it comes back to the same place, so don't worry that you might
make a wrong turn. The trail becomes very steep, with some high
step-ups. There are many manzanitas.

As you gain in elevation, the views of the surrounding mountains and valleys gives you a forecast of the views to come.
Vegetation changes to include alligator juniper and scrub oak.

After a seemingly endless climb through the manzanita and
around boulders, the trail changes abruptly, turning left and dropping

down into an exceptionally pretty area. It reaches a deep drainage and then climbs gradually along the left side of the drainage. Much of the year water is flowing in this area. The trail is covered by a canopy of trees. Grapevines remind me of the eastern mountains, where as a child we cut the vines and swung far out over ravines. This could be done here, although the boulders below would be dangerous if the vine broke. Half way up the drainage, a large pile of rocks makes an excellent lunch spot. In spring, wild geraniums and other flowers add to the beauty.

Near the head of the drainage on the right is the first ponderosa pine, the first of many to come. Past the ponderosa, the trail turns to the right and crosses a small drainage before turning left and away from the large ravine. Here you begin to climb steeply again, and the canopy is gone as the view opens up and the trail approaches Happy Valley Saddle. Now the views are amazing. Blue mountains fade away in the distance. At the top of the saddle, you get a good view of your goal, Rincon Peak. It really looks impossible that you can be on top of this mountain in a few miles.

At the saddle the trail drops slightly to the intersection with the Miller Creek and Heartbreak Ridge trails. Turn left at this intersection .5 miles to the Rincon Peak Trail sign. Here you will turn left for the final 3.2 miles to the top of Rincon Peak. It takes three to five hours to reach this point.

An interesting side trip and an excellent spot for camping, should you decide to do this trail as a backpack, is to continue one-quarter of a mile past the Rincon Peak Trail intersection to the Happy Valley Campground. The campground has three sites that must be reserved through the Saguaro National Monument Rincon Unit headquarters in Tucson. It also has a grill and established fire rings, as well as a welcome restroom! A stream runs through the campground and almost always has at least small pools of water. Tall ponderosa shade the area and carpet the ground with needles. Happy Valley Campground is truly one of the gems of the Rincons.

We'll assume that you are doing this trail as an all-out day effort and continue 3.2 miles up the Rincon Peak Trail to the summit. Past the intersection, the trail climbs slightly and then levels off. For nearly a mile the trail drops into and out of a series of small ravines. There are many alligator junipers and the ever-present manzanitas. The trail is still pleasant, and you may wonder where the difficult part is—don't worry, it will come soon enough. As the trail begins to climb, it crosses a large side drainage and shortly another one. Most of the year there will be some water trickling down the rocks in these drainages. By now you are in the open, where the views are astounding. Walk past a particularly thick stand of manzanita, and you can see the western end of the city of Tucson. As you climb, more and more of the city will be visible. Past this point the trail begins to climb more steeply, with occasional switchbacks and some long, steep climbs. Always the views are excellent. As you look toward Tucson, you can see Tanque Verde Ridge and catch a glimpse of the Catalina Mountains.

The trail drops in and out of several deep ravines, climbing steeply between them. By now you are in ponderosa country. Along the side of the mountain you come to a small spring. A circle of rocks contains the actual spring, and the area surrounding the spring is covered with tiny green cloverlike plants. Past the spring you see your first Douglas fir. This is a beautiful section, not too steep, under a canopy of ponderosa pine and Douglas fir. The trail is soft and the climb imperceptible for a distance. This cannot last if you are to reach the top.

Less than a mile from the summit, you reach a sign that reads Foot Trail Only, No Stock. This marks the beginning of the final ascent on the peak. Be consoled by the views, which are spectacular. It is steep; there are some switchbacks, but not enough for my liking. The trail is slippery, often covered with fallen branches and trees. A small patch of aspen grow near the top, one of the few stands of aspen in the Rincons. But persevere and you will make it. Near the top you actually go down a few steps, and there on a shelf is the trail register. You can see by the small number of signatures that not too many make it.

Unfortunately, this is not the top. It is two hundred yards more of steep rock scramble to the summit. The trail is not always distinct in this section, but the only way is up. Work your way carefully from rock to rock, and you will be there quickly.

The top is worth the climb. Hope that you have a clear day after all this effort. It takes the average hiker two to three hours to do the final 3.2 miles. Not much grows on the top. A few manzanitas and, surprisingly, a number of hedgehog cacti. The wind can be very strong. A ten-foot-high cairn marks the actual summit. A summit register is anchored in a metal box near the summit. Should there be any sign of a storm, get off the summit. As you can imagine, this is a target for lightning. Hopefully you can remain here for a while and with the aid of a map pick out the mountain ranges you can see. On a clear day you can see Baboquivari Peak, Kitt Peak, Mount Wrightson, the Catalinas, and far into Mexico.

If you are doing this as a day hike, don't linger too long. The way down is treacherous and takes almost as long as the way up.

The Santa Catalina Mountains

In A.D. 900 Hohokam women ground mesquite beans in summer camps high in the canyons of the Santa Catalina Mountains while their men hunted. Bedrock mortars and petroglyphs remain as evidence.

The Hohokam were gone and the Pima Indians were living in the Tucson Basin by the time the Jesuit priest, Father Kino, established his mission at San Xavier del Bac in the late 1600s. Kino referred to the mountains to the north and east as the Santa Caterina Mountains, possibly in honor of St. Catherine. In time the name changed to the Santa Catalina Mountains.

By the early 1800s, Apache Indians hunted and camped in the Catalinas and occasionally raided the settlements and the mission near Tucson. To protect their missions and route to California, the Spaniards built a fort on the site of what is today downtown Tucson. Apaches attacked the fort unsuccessfully, and the Spaniards survived until the Mexican War of Independence shifted ownership of Tucson to Mexico in 1821.

By 1854, when the United States secured possession with the Gadsden Purchase, Anglos with the gleam of gold in their eye began to move into Tucson. They built trails into the Catalinas, looking for gold, then silver and copper.

Others were interested in the Catalinas. Sara Plummer Lemmon and her husband came to the Catalinas in 1880. Botanists on their honeymoon, they rode horseback up from Oracle, guided by rancher E. O. Stratton. On the highest peak, the three carved their initials on a large pine and christened the peak Mount Lemmon, in honor of Sara. The name stuck and today the 9,157-foot high point of the Santa Catalinas is still called Mount Lemmon.

By 1891 there were those who thought these mountains should be protected, and Congress authorized the president to withdraw certain lands from the public domain. In 1902 the Catalina Forest Preserve was created. A conservationist president, Theodore Roosevelt, organized the National Forest Service in 1905, and by 1908 the Coronado National Forest was born.

More trails were built into the high country, and Tucsonans camped there in the summer. Some leased land and built cabins. Much discussion was devoted to building a road up the mountain.

By 1920 a rough road had been carved up to the top from Oracle, but Tucsonans wanted a "short road" from their side of the mountain.

After much maneuvering by Frank Hitchcock, editor and publisher of the Tucson *Citizen,* Secretary of Agriculture Henry A. Wallace approved a twenty-five-mile, two-lane surfaced road up to the village of Summerhaven. The federal government would foot the bill, and it would be built by prisoners. Construction began in 1933 and inched up the mountain. It was not completed until 1951. The road was named in honor of the man who got it all going but did not live to see it completed.

To protect the mountains from further development, the Pusch Ridge Wilderness Area was created in 1978 under the endangered American Wilderness Act. In all, 56,933 acres, encompassing nearly the entire front range, are now closed to future development and all motorized vehicles. Mountain bikes are not permitted. The only way to get to the heart of this spectacular area is on foot or horseback.

There are eleven trails in the Catalinas described in this guide. The Catalinas are rugged mountains, and none of the hikes are categorized as "easy." If you have never been in the Catalinas and want an easy introduction, hike the first three miles of the Pima Canyon Trail. Hutch's Pool is also a good introductory hike. Make sure you are in good hiking condition before attempting the trails rated "extremely difficult."

West Fork of Sabino Trail to Hutch's Pool

General Description
> *A pleasant combination tram ride and hike to a beautiful pool of Sabino Creek*

Difficulty
> *Moderate, steep switchbacks for first .8 miles*

Best time of year to hike
> *Early spring, late fall, winter*

Length
> *4.1 miles*

Elevation
> *3500 feet at the end of the road; 3900 feet at Hutch's Pool*

Miles to trailhead from Speedway/Campbell intersection
> *11.1*

Directions to trailhead from Speedway/Campbell intersection
> *Go east on Speedway 5 miles to Wilmot Road. Turn left. Wilmot becomes Tanque Verde at the Pima intersection. Continue on Tanque Verde to Sabino Canyon Road. Turn left and follow the signs to the Sabino Canyon Visitor Center parking lot. The trailhead is 3.8 miles from the visitor center at the end of the Sabino Canyon Road.*

In the early 1940s, Don Everett, an English and Latin teacher at the Southern Arizona School for Boys (now Fenster School of Arizona), took his students on horseback rides into the Catalinas. Whenever he would pass a prominent landmark for the first time, Everett would name it after a student in his group. On a ride from Sabino Canyon to Mount Lemmon, Everett passed what he called "the most beautiful pool in the Catalinas." A student from Chicago, Roger Hutchinson, was on the ride, and Everett named the pool Hutch's Pool. It is still the most beautiful pool in the Catalinas.

The switchbacks at the north end of Sabino Canyon Road are the starting point for several trails leading into the Catalinas, including the west fork of Sabino Trail, which passes Hutch's Pool.

Hutch's Pool, Santa Catalina Mountains

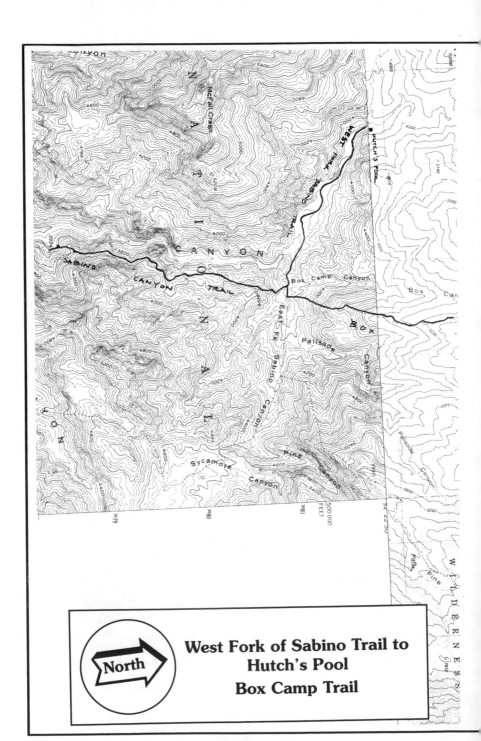

West Fork of Sabino Trail to Hutch's Pool

Box Camp Trail

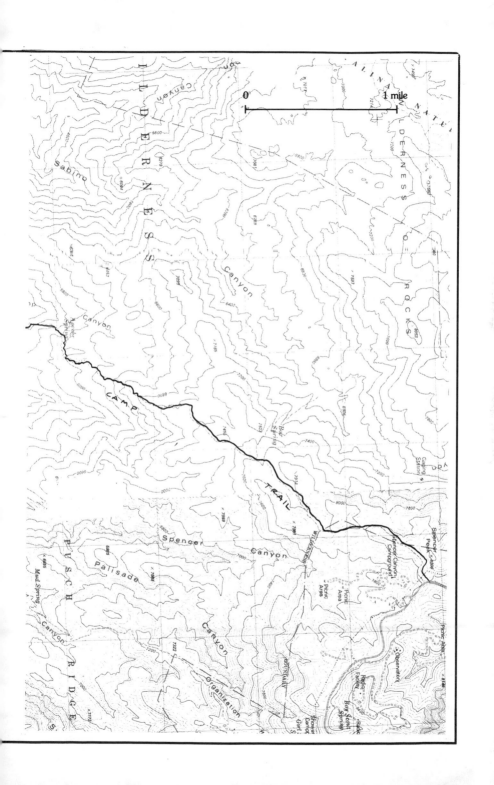

The quickest way to reach the trailhead is by the Sabino Canyon tram (five dollars per person); however, some hardy hikers prefer to walk the additional 3.8 miles to the switchbacks.

The trail climbs steeply for .8 miles. After half a mile the Phoneline Trail cuts off to the right. This is a popular tram-hike loop for people who ride the tram up and hike the 4 miles back down the Phoneline Trail to lower Sabino Canyon.

A few more switchbacks and the trail levels off along the top of the ridge. The city is now out of sight. To the left and far below is Sabino Creek. There are a few uphill, rocky spots, but for the most part the trail is a gradual and easy climb until it begins meandering its way along the side of the ridge down to Sabino Basin.

After a mile and a half, the trail makes a sharp curve to the right and begins descending quickly. At this curve there is a partially barricaded side trail to the left that leads to a lookout point providing an excellent view of Sabino Creek. The view is worth the short side trip.

As you continue on the main trail and approach Sabino Basin, you can appreciate why it is such a popular area. A lush drainage where Mexican blue oak and Arizona sycamore flourish, the basin is a crossroads for hikers en route to the backcountry of the Catalinas. A metal sign gives directions and mileage to several points. It is twelve miles to Mount Lemmon, 2.5 miles back to Sabino Road, and 1.6 miles ahead to Hutch's Pool.

Blue jays claim this territory, and if you sit down for a snack or lunch, a jay will watch to see if you drop a crumb. Toss one, and you hear the chatter of birds. Soon an entire flock is sitting in the trees. Finally one gets brave enough to get the crumb, and the entire bunch heads after him.

When you tire of the jay performance and continue ahead to the pool, you first leave the drainage, cross a rocky, sandy area, and enter a meadow, hiking away from Sabino Creek for nearly a mile. A level open field to the left is a popular campground. Archaeologists of the future may have a field day here, sifting through fire rings littered with the trash of the twentieth century. A quarter of a mile past the field, the trail begins to parallel Sabino Creek, going along a narrow ledge where a slip could give you a pretty good tumble. Shortly the trail descends into the drainage of, and then crosses, Sabino Creek. Although there are large boulders to hop on, the crossing could be treacherous in times of heavy runoff.

Cairns mark the trail, which now follows the left, or west, side of the creek. After a quarter of a mile, several paths to the right lead down to the creek. The first side trail leads to a large pool, which is a lovely spot but is not the actual Hutch's Pool. Hutch's Pool can be reached either by descending the next path farther along the trail and boulder hopping upstream or by descending the third path, which is fairly steep and leads along the side of the creek past a large camping site.

Hutch's Pool is long and narrow and has a waterfall at the north end. It is easy to understand why so many people make the effort to hike the 4.1 miles required to reach this spectacular pool.

Unfortunately, some of the people who hike here are apparently oblivious to its beauty and leave their trash behind. I have always been curious as to why people who are perfectly willing to carry full cans of soda, beans, and spaghetti to camp are then unwilling to carry the much lighter, empty cans out. Since human behavior will not change, a good idea is to bring a trash bag and carry out some of the litter when you leave.

The pool looks like the perfect swimming pool, but hidden rocks can be dangerous, and diving should not be attempted. Lives have been lost by people diving recklessly into the pool.

It takes two to three hours to reach Hutch's Pool, depending on how long you linger along the way. If you care to explore a little further, there are smaller pools a few hundred yards upstream.

Box Camp Trail

General Description
An excellent hike beginning in ponderosa pine and ending in saguaro cactus that requires a car shuttle

Difficulty
Difficult, mostly continuous steep downhill

Best time of year to hike
Spring, fall

Length
9.6 miles to Sabino Canyon tram

Elevation
8050 feet at Mount Lemmon trailhead; 3700 feet at Sabino Basin

Miles to trailhead from Speedway/Campbell intersection
32.9 from intersection to trailhead (does not include leaving a car at Sabino Canyon Visitor Center parking lot)

Directions to trailhead from Speedway/Campbell intersection
Leave one car at the Sabino Canyon Visitor Center parking lot. Go east on Speedway to Wilmot Road. Turn left on Wilmot Road. Wilmot becomes Tanque Verde. Continue on Tanque Verde until Sabino Canyon Road. Turn left on Sabino Canyon Road until the Visitor Center parking lot, which is on the right. Get in the second car and go back to Tanque Verde. Turn left until the Catalina Highway. Turn left on the Catalina Highway until .8 miles past milepost 21. The parking area for the Box Camp Trail is on the left, past Spencer Canyon Road and before milepost 22. The sign indicating the trailhead is on the hill, to the right of the small parking area. (This car shuttle can be avoided if you can talk someone into driving you up to the trailhead.)

The Box Camp Trail was an early pack route to the high country of the Catalinas. In the days before air-conditioning, Tucsonans rode horses up this trail to summer cabins or camps to escape the desert heat.

Tucson from Box Camp Trail

The trail, which today connects the Mount Lemmon Highway to the Sabino Canyon tram, is one of the most dramatic trails in the Tucson area. The trail begins almost a mile past milepost 21 at 8,500 feet. It ends after 7.1 miles of nearly continuous downhill in Sabino Basin at thirty-seven hundred feet. From Sabino Basin it is 2.5 miles to the head of the Sabino Canyon Road where, if you make it by 4:00 P.M., you can catch a tram to the Visitor Center parking lot.

Assuming you have arranged transportation according to the directions above and have enough money for the tram, you're ready to begin. The trailhead is on the right side of the parking area and is marked by a metal sign.

The trail begins with two hundred yards of uphill before leveling out at the power line. It goes through an old burn area that has regrown and is covered with large ferns, then drops to the west side of the ridge and switchbacks through tall ponderosa pines to the head of a small stream. The trail continues along the bottom of a ravine, crossing and recrossing the stream several times. As you progress downhill the stream gets larger. If there is water, which there will be in early spring, this is a lovely area, with small waterfalls along the way.

There are several fallen trees across the trail, including a large one that has fallen lengthwise just as the trail begins to recross the stream. Hikers have beaten out a path around the tree and up the side of the canyon to rejoin the trail. The trail continues down the side of the mountain through a carpet of ferns and under the tall ponderosa pines.

Partway down, a sign on a tree indicates that Box Spring is .3 miles on a side trail to the right. This was the site of the old Box Camp, a place to water your horses, rest, and perhaps camp overnight.

The main trail continues down for another quarter of a mile before emerging from the thick pine forest into a more open area with scrub oak and manzanita. From here on, the views of the city and of the nearby canyons will be awesome. Notice Thimble Peak, the prominent thimble-shaped landmark above Sabino Canyon. Before your hike is over, you will be looking up at the Thimble.

The now-rocky trail goes down the top of the ridge between Spencer Canyon on the left and Box Camp Canyon on the right. About half way down this ridge is an area that looks like it was at one time cleared for a helicopter landing. The trail crosses this cleared area and continues down the mountain. There has by now been an almost total change in vegetation. An hour ago you were in a thick, cool pine forest. Now you are hiking through manzanita, scrub oak, and a few piñon pine.

At this point, for a short time, the trail becomes hard to follow. Look carefully for cairns and avoid side trails that are blocked by a row of rocks. What is confusing is that it appears that you should head in a more direct route toward the Thimble, when actually the general direction of the trail is to drop to the right, or northwest, and circle around the point of the ridge. As you continue to descend, the trail bears to the right and switchbacks steeply down through loose rocks before leveling out in a brushy area. The manzanita is so thick that in one area it has formed a tunnel across the trail. Although it is quite overgrown, the trail through the brush is relatively easy to follow.

The trail approaches Box Camp Canyon and then turns left, or southeast, and circles the ridge. Here an interesting rock formation comes into view. It is a long, high sheaf of rocks that has many balanced rocks on top. Just before reaching this sheaf of rocks there is a pretty area known as Apache Spring. The trail crosses a small stream, and there are some large pines to provide shade. Most of

the year there will be at least a little water and a number of wildflowers growing in this area. If, in fact, the Apache Indians did
camp here, it is easy to understand why.

Across the stream the trail changes in character. It goes to the
right of the sheaf of rocks and switchbacks its way down through an
area covered with large boulders. There are some pine trees and a
number of large scrub oaks, breaking for a while the intense sun of
the previous part of the trail.

After coming out of this boulder-strewn section, you are close
to Box Camp Canyon. There is a faint trail where other hikers have
gone into the canyon. The correct route is to parallel the canyon for
few hundred yards before veering left for a short level area that
gives your legs a break from the constant downhill. As you go along
the side of the ridge, you can clearly see Sabino Basin, distinguished by the line of green trees. By now you are hiking way
below the Thimble. The trail circles to the northeast and provides a
good view of Palisades Canyon, where, if there is enough water,
there is a large waterfall.

This section is more open, with just a few trees (mainly scrub
oak), but with plenty of the nastiest plant in the Catalinas: amoles,
better known as shindaggers, cover the area. At one point the trail
appears to head back uphill and toward the mountains. Don't worry!
It soon makes a sharp right and heads directly for Sabino Basin
through a short level area.

Just past this level area you come to a long series of switchbacks that will lead you to the basin. Here the saguaro appear again
and by now you are at about the thirty-five hundred-foot level. The
saguaro in this area are large and healthy.

At the bottom of the switchbacks you level off briefly and then
enter the cool, shady Sabino Basin. After crossing a creek that
nearly always has water, you come to a sign that reads Mount
Lemmon Highway 7.1. Here you turn right and go through a thick
stand of trees to a major intersection. At the intersection are
two signs indicating the directions of several trails that meet in the
basin.

Directly across the creek from the signs, the trail climbs steeply
out of Sabino Basin for the first half-mile, and then circles the
canyon for approximately one and one-half miles until coming to
the switchbacks that look down on the road. Usually you can see
the tram coming up the road. It seems to me that this last half-mile

of switchbacks down to the tram is the longest portion of the trail! When the tram arrives, give the driver your money and hop on board.

Invariably, as you obviously look a little worse for wear, some-one will say, "Where did you come from?" It is fun to see their reaction when you say, "Mount Lemmon!"

Blackett's Ridge Trail

General Description
A short hike on a ridge between Sabino and Bear canyons with spectacular views of Tucson and the canyons

Difficulty
Moderate, steep for first mile

Best time of year to hike
Early spring, late fall, winter

Length
2.3 miles

Elevation
2700 feet to 4409 feet

Miles to trailhead from Speedway/Campbell intersection
11.1

Directions to trailhead from Speedway/Campbell intersection
Go east on Speedway 5 miles to Wilmot Road. Turn left. Wilmot becomes Tanque Verde at the Pima intersection. Continue on Tanque Verde to Sabino Canyon Road. Turn left and follow the signs to the Sabino Canyon Visitor Center parking lot. The trailhead can be reached by tram or by walking .8 miles across the parking lot and on the road.

Blackett's Ridge Trail is one of the best little hikes in the Tucson area. It is not on the official maps, and its existence is carried by word of mouth. Blackett's Ridge is the ridge that separates Sabino and Bear canyons. The ridge was named by Don Everett, a teacher at the Southern Arizona School for Boys, after one of his students. In 1937 Everett made the first ascent of the ridge on horseback, accompanied by Hill Blackett, Jr., a student from Winnetka, Illinois. From that day the ridge has been called Blackett's Ridge.

You can reach the trailhead by riding the Bear Canyon tram, or, if you prefer, by walking on the wide path that crosses the desert from the southeast corner of the parking lot to the road. When you reach the road, continue walking to the right, passing to the right of the restrooms, across the bridge, and again to the right to the Seven Falls Trail sign. If you are riding the tram, tell the

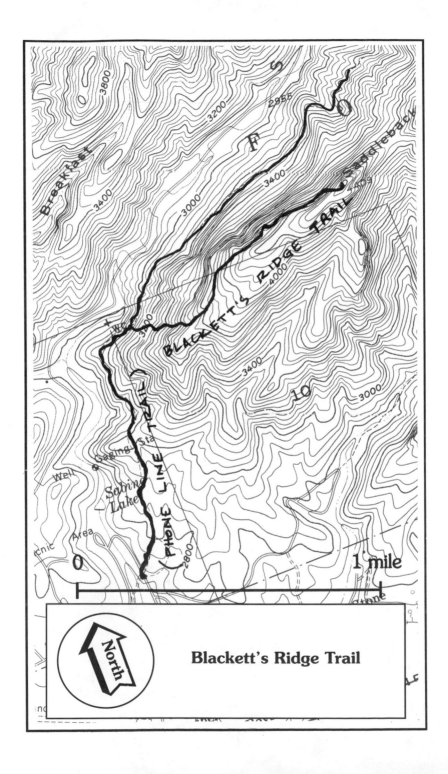

Blackett's Ridge Trail

Blackett's Ridge

driver that you want off across the first bridge by that sign. To return by tram, you must be at the Stop 2 sign for pickup. This sign is at the intersection back across the bridge and up the hill for a short distance.

The trail begins on the left of the Seven Falls Trail sign. After one hundred yards, there is a signed trail intersection. Take the Phoneline Trail to the left. This trail follows the route of an old phone line to Mount Lemmon and is popular with joggers, who like to run up the trail and down the road, and hikers, who ride the tram up Sabino Canyon and hike down the trail.

There is a very gradual elevation gain on smooth trail, through the typical vegetation of this elevation. After .6 miles you come to a turnoff to the right that leads to Blackett's Ridge. Since this is not an official Forest Service trail, there is no sign; but most of the time there will be a cairn. It takes twenty minutes of leisurely hiking to reach this turnoff, which is well used and easy to spot.

Straight ahead and high above is Blackett's Ridge. The Phoneline Trail continues up the canyon, and the trail to Blackett's Ridge begins to switchback up the ridge. After about one-quarter of a mile, Sabino Canyon is visible, and you can see the tram. If the wind is right, you can hear the narration of the tram guide. Sabino Creek is visible, as is a small dam. In 1910 and again in the 1930s, private companies and government agencies made serious proposals to dam part of Sabino Canyon for use as Tucson's water and electric supply. Had any of these projects materialized, the views from Blackett's Ridge would be quite different!

The switchbacks become very steep and shorter as you come to the top of the front part of the trail. You level off for a short distance and wind around to the south side of the ridge. The Santa Ritas are now directly in front of you. In winter, which is the best time to do this hike, Mount Wrightson is usually snow covered, as are the Rincon Mountains to the east. As the trail continues, the switchbacks get even steeper, and soon the road leading to Bear Canyon is visible. A tram runs hourly to the popular Seven Falls trailhead.

You quickly come to the first of several good lookout points. It is as if you were driving through the Rocky Mountains and coming to signs indicating Scenic Pullout. You can sit and observe the valley below at several such "pullouts" along the first part of this trail. You can easily make it to the first lookout in forty-five minutes.

As you recover from the steep climb, survey the sights. The greens of the Loew's Ventana Canyon Resort golf course are in sharp contrast to the desert. You can also see and hear the Tucson Rod and Gun Club Rifle Range. By now the parking lot of Sabino Canyon is a small asphalt square.

Past this first lookout, the trail continues gaining elevation. By the time you have reached the fourth lookout, you have an excellent view up Sabino Canyon and into the heart of the Catalinas. The towers on Radio Ridge stand out. The dark covering on top is ponderosa pine, another ecosystem altogether. You then come to a long, smooth saddle, and you know you are definitely on a narrow ridge between two canyons. On the right are the Rincons and Santa Ritas and on the left are the Catalinas and Sabino Canyon.

As you cross the saddle, the trail again becomes rocky and climbs toward what looks like the high point of the ridge. Topped by a big pile of rocks, this high point is the first of three false summits. The trail is distinct and climbs gradually, going to the left of what appeared to be the high point.

As the trail ascends toward a second apparent summit, it bears slightly to the right and becomes quite steep. The area on the right was burned several years ago, and many of the saguaros show evidence of the fire. They are black around the bottom but still green at the top. They appear to be alive, but only time will tell if they survive.

Straight ahead is a magnificent view of Thimble Peak, at 5,323 feet, the highest point in the canyon. A side trail to the left leads to the third false summit, where the Forest Service maintains an antenna for communication purposes. The views from up here are great, but the actual summit of Blackett's Ridge is still a few hundred yards ahead.

The trail ends abruptly. Climbing expertise is required for any further exploration of the ridge. Extreme caution must be exercised in this area. The cliffs to the left, called the Acropolis Cliffs by the tram drivers, drop four hundred feet into Sabino Canyon. A misstep could be tragic.

However dangerous the summit of Blackett's Ridge, it does provide literally breathtaking views into Sabino Canyon. The Phoneline Trail has become a narrow ribbon. The now-tiny trams traverse the road, their drivers introducing tourists to the diversity of Sabino Canyon. As you sit quietly, you can hear the rush of water in Sabino Creek, occasionally mingled with the voices of people. Birds dive down the cliffs, and occasionally deer can be spotted as they head to the water below. The four mountain ranges that surround Tucson make an unforgettable panorama.

It takes about an hour to return to the parking lot. The Blackett's Ridge hike is a good morning's workout and one that you will return to many times.

Note: This hike is sometimes referred to as Saddleback.

Esperero Trail

General Description
A long hike over rugged terrain, with dramatic views of the Tucson Valley

Difficulty
Extremely difficult

Best time of year to hike
Early spring, late fall

Length
8.4 miles

Elevation
2700 feet to 4409 feet

Miles to trailhead from Speedway/Campbell intersection
11.1 to Visitor Center parking lot

Directions to trailhead from Speedway/Campbell intersection
Go east on Speedway 5 miles to Wilmot Road. Turn left. Wilmot becomes Tanque Verde at the Pima intersection. Continue on Tanque Verde to Sabino Canyon Road. Turn left and follow the signs to the Sabino Canyon Visitor Center parking lot. It is .7 miles up the Sabino Canyon Road to the trailhead.

Esperero Trail begins in Sabino Canyon and climbs 8.4 miles to a twenty-five-foot opening in the crest of a ridge called the Window. Elevation at the trailhead is 2,850 feet. At the end of the trail you'll be at seven thousand feet and be able to see most of Tucson. The trail, originally known as the Dixie Saddle Trail, was constructed in 1924 by Forest Service workers as a trail for use by horseback riders. It was described in an early newspaper account as a trail on which "natural wonders meet the gaze at every turn." The reason the name was changed to *Esperero,* Spanish for "hopeful," is unknown.

Park in the visitor lot at Sabino Canyon and begin walking up the asphalt road into the canyon. At .7 miles, past the currently unmanned information booth, you will see a sign on the left indicating the Cactus picnic area. Immediately past the sign, turn left on

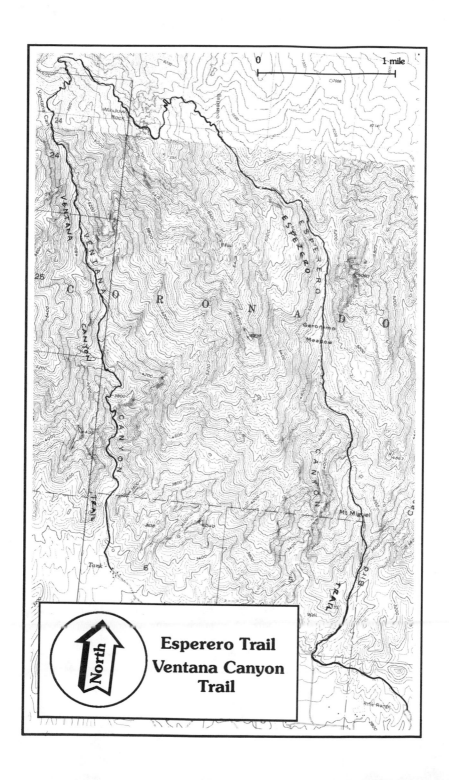

Esperero Trail
Ventana Canyon
Trail

Esperero Trail

the road and veer slightly right until you see a rock with a water spigot. Right next to the rock is the trailhead. A large sign indicates Esperero Trail.

After about .8 miles, you will come to a picnic table with a trail sign on the right. Follow the sign to the right and continue uphill until you reach a signed trail intersection. To the right is a trail dropping into Sabino Canyon. You want to turn left. As you look backward, you realize that you have already gained considerable elevation. From this spot you can see the observatory on Kitt Peak and much of the Tucson Valley.

Beyond the intersection, the trail levels and then drops into Rattlesnake Canyon. Rattlesnakes deter some people from hiking in the Catalinas. True, Arizona does have more rattlers than any other state in the Union, but in twenty years of hiking these mountains, I have only seen two. If you see or hear a rattler, stay away from it, and be familiar with the proper treatment procedures given in the front of this guide.

The next part of the trail can be confusing. Where there is danger of getting off the trail, low barriers of sticks and stones block the way. Also, cairns (small piles of rocks) mark the trail in critical spots. It is still possible to go astray and come close to the Tucson Rod and Gun Club's Sabino Rifle Range.

Although the sound of gunfire is disconcerting, there is no danger from the target range, according to Edward Owen, senior firearms instructor at the Rod and Gun Club. "There is no possibility of being struck by a stray bullet fired at any of the target stations on the range. The backstops, which are over twenty feet tall, stop all bullets fired down range," Owen explained. Admittedly, the sound of bullets is not what you go into the wilderness for, but be assured that the target range is safe, and after about two miles of hiking you won't be able to hear any shots.

After about a mile of strenuous climbing, you level off and then make a sharp descent into Bird Canyon. Here the trail crosses a short section of private land. The boundary is clearly marked with a warning that the privilege of hiking can be revoked if hikers do not stay on the trail.

The vegetation along the trail thus far is typical of the three thousand- to four thousand-foot elevation range in the Sonoran Desert: saguaro, barrel, prickly pear, and cholla cacti; ocotillos; mesquite and palo verde trees; and assorted shrubs, including creosote bush and brittlebush. You may spot deer, javelina, or coyote; and small lizards scatter as you hike. If you are interested in identifying those lizards, the National Forest Visitor Center in Sabino Canyon has an information sheet that identifies twelve species. The problem is getting them to hold still long enough for you to identify them!

The trail climbs gradually out of Bird Canyon, then drops into a deep side drainage. A series of steep step-ups makes this one of the more difficult sections of Esperero, as it hugs the side of the drainage for nearly a mile. It is also one of the prettiest sections, with many large saguaros clinging miraculously to what appears to be barren rock.

Once you come out of the drainage, the real hike begins. It is here that shindaggers make their appearance. This wicked plant has sharp daggers at shin level and attacks anyone who wanders too far off the trail.

This one-quarter-mile section of the trail between the drainage and the ridgetop has been nicknamed "cardiac gap" by local hikers. Don't let the nickname deter you—it's not *that* bad! A series of switchbacks get you to the top of the ridge. Go slowly, and enjoy the view as the city below spreads out across the valley. It's fun to pick out landmarks. The flashing tower lights of Tucson Electric Power's substation are easy to spot. Persist, and before you realize it, you are on top of cardiac gap. It takes the average hiker two and one-half to three hours to reach this point, a distance of approximately three miles.

The ridge is an excellent lunch spot. Turn your back on the city, and the magnificent Catalinas seem to go on forever. Cathedral Rock is the dominant formation of this part of the range. Below, providing there has been enough rainfall, there is a large waterfall where Esperero Canyon empties into the basin. From this point it takes about two hours to return to the Sabino Canyon parking lot. This is a good turnaround point for your first attempt at Esperero Trail.

If you choose to continue, Esperero has a lot more to offer. The trail drops down on the north side of the ridge slightly, climbs steadily for about one-quarter of a mile, and then levels out and circles the basin. Scrub oak, juniper, piñon pine, and manzanita grow at this elevation, approximately five thousand feet. Many of the deep red-stemmed manzanita appear to have died. According to Dale Mance, trail supervisor for the Santa Catalina Ranger District of the Coronado National Forest, the manzanita's leaves are brown due to the severe lack of rainfall for the past year. "It is possible," Mance stated, "that they are not dead and will revive with adequate rainfall. We won't know for another year."

Less than a mile from the ridge, the trail passes a large out-cropping of rocks on the left and enters Geronimo Meadow. Geronimo Meadow is not a meadow by most definitions. The "meadow" is a level area filled with manzanita and a few pine. There is a good camping spot, complete with a large fire ring and a log to sit on. Although environmentally aware campers do not leave evidence of their stay, there are many such fire rings in the Cata-linas. The spot is used frequently, as evidenced by the utter lack of fear displayed by a very friendly roadrunner who came into our camp recently and demanded food. When we obeyed the warnings not to feed wildlife, he scolded us with a clucking noise, perched himself on a rock, and unsuccessfully tried to wait us out.

Beyond the meadow the trail drops sharply into Esperero Canyon. A creek flows sporadically, mostly in early spring. The trail follows the creek, crisscrossing it several times. If you think you're off the trail, look for cairns. A heavy stand of tall oak trees shades the trail, and this part of the hike is quite pleasant.

One mile upstream and you come to Mormon Spring. A sign indicates a concrete tank off to the right that, in all except the driest season, is filled with water. There are also several pools above the spring that nearly always contain water. Don't drink from either source unless you have a way to purify the water.

Beyond Mormon Spring it's another half mile to Bridal Veil Falls. The trail is overgrown, difficult to follow, and very steep in places, but the waterfalls at the end make it all worthwhile. About fifty feet tall and surrounded by towering ponderosa pines, it resembles a bride's veil when sufficient rainfall creates a spray. Even when there has been very little rain, there is usually a trickle, enough for a refreshing shower on a hot afternoon. At the waterfall you will have hiked five and one-half miles and gained 2,450 feet—a respectable day's hike.

Only very well-conditioned, experienced hikers should continue the final 2.9 miles to the Window. In winter the trail could be icy or covered with snow, and the short days may not allow time to return before dark. If you do continue, expect some major climbing above Bridal Veil Falls and a final sharp descent before you stand in the

Window at seven thousand feet (a shorter route to the Window is via the Ventana Canyon Trail).

In its entirety, Esperero is one of the most difficult trails in the Catalinas. It is also, as you will see in your view from the Window, one of the most rewarding.

Ventana Canyon Trail

General Description

A challenging hike through one of the most beautiful canyons in the front range of the Catalinas

Difficulty

Difficult, some areas of steep climbing

Best time of year to hike

Spring, fall

Length

6.4 miles

Elevation

2950 feet to 7000 feet

Miles to trailhead from Speedway/Campbell intersection

12.2

Directions to trailhead from Speedway/Campbell intersection

Go east on Speedway 5 miles to Wilmot Road. Turn left. Wilmot becomes Tanque Verde at the Pima intersection. Continue on Tanque Verde to Sabino Canyon Road. Turn left on Sabino Canyon Road 3.7 miles to the intersection of Kolb Road. Turn left on Kolb Road for 3.4 miles to the entrance to Loew's Ventana Canyon Resort. Turn right .1 miles until you reach the employees' parking lot, which is on the left just before you reach the resort. Park in the employees' lot. Put a sign on your dash reading Hiking Ventana Canyon Trail.

As you look toward the Catalinas from the Grant-Campbell area, if the light is just right, you can see a tiny hole at the top of the mountain in about the middle of the range. That "tiny" hole is in a large rock fin at the crest of a ridge far above Ventana Canyon. It is an oval opening approximately fifteen feet high and twenty-five feet wide, known as the "Window," or *Ventana* in Spanish.

It is a challenging 6.4 miles up the Ventana Canyon Trail to the Window. Beginning at thirty-two hundred feet, amid saguaro and mesquite, you eventually reach seven thousand feet, where ponderosa pines tower above you. The nearly thirteen-mile round trip will take most of the day.

View east through the Window, Ventana Canyon Trail

Even though it is one of the most beautiful trails in the Catalinas, the Ventana Canyon Trail is infrequently used. One reason is
the maze of instructions you have to work through just to get to the
trailhead. As you must cross land belonging to the privately owned
Flying V Ranch to reach the trailhead, it is important that you call
the Flying V at 299-4372 and let the owners know the day you will
be hiking and the number in your party. It is all right to leave the
information on the recording if no one answers.

As is noted above, parking for the Ventana Canyon trailhead is
in the employee lot of the Loew's Ventana Canyon Resort. To reach
the trailhead, walk back to Kolb Road. Turn right on Kolb Road and
walk a short distance to the Canyon View at Ventana apartment
complex. Turn right on Canyon Crest Drive into the complex. Go
straight on Canyon Crest Drive until the Leasing Office sign. Turn
left at this intersection. Turn right at the recreation building and
tennis court area. Turn left at the end of the tennis courts. Straight
ahead and on the right, immediately past apartment 9150, there is
a small parking area on the right. The trail begins to the left of this
parking area.

In two hundred yards you will come to the Flying V warning
sign reminding you that their property is not to be crossed without
permission. (Remember this sign as the point to turn right off the
road on your return trip; otherwise, you may mistakenly continue
on the road and end up staring at an eight-foot chain link fence.)
At this sign the trail bears left and soon becomes a road. Just
beyond an open area is the gate and signs indicating that you have
reached the Ventana Canyon trailhead.

The entrance to Ventana Canyon is spectacular, with steep cliffs
rising on each side. The first mile of the trail follows the creek,
crossing it several times. The creek is dry most of the year, but in
late winter and spring it is usually running. After about a mile and a
half, you begin to climb out of the bottom of the canyon, up a
series of steep switchbacks. At intervals there are concrete slabs
across this section of the trail that, while they prevent erosion, make
walking more treacherous. This portion of the trail has splendid
views of the city below and the ever-present Mount Wrightson south
of Tucson. As you top the first set of switchbacks, you can see the
apartment complex where you began and part of the golf course of
the resort.

Over the crest of the hill, you drop down into an area known as Maiden Pools. This is a beautiful section of the canyon. If the stream is running, there is a large waterfall, nearly fifty feet high, as you approach the pools. Behind the waterfall is a series of pools, a few large enough for swimming. It is easy to visualize how the area got its name—a beautiful maiden would look right at home here, sunbathing amid the pools and lush vegetation. Flowers and grasses grow in abundance. Large Mexican blue oaks provide shade, and there are many perfect picnic spots. This is a good turnaround point for a half day hike, as it takes less than two hours to reach this point.

If you plan to continue to the Window, be aware that at Maiden Pools it is very easy to get off the trail because there are many side trails that lead down to the pools. The trail to the Window stays above the pool area. If you take a side trail, be sure to come back up the same trail you went down.

Above Maiden Pools the trail is quite confusing for about a mile. It crosses the creek several times, and parts are very brushy. Watch carefully for cairns that indicate direction.

About one mile past Maiden Pools, you come to a second pool area, smaller than Maiden Pools but equally pretty. Several large Arizona sycamores, distinguished by the white sections of peeling bark, grow in this area.

Past the sycamores, and to the west side of the creek, is a steep section where you gain elevation rapidly without the aid of switchbacks. About half way up this section is a large smooth rock with two deep bedrock mortars, circular depressions caused by Indian women grinding mesquite beans or other legumes. This is evidence that at one time, nearly one thousand years ago, Hohokam Indians camped and hunted in this canyon.

A few steps past the mortars look to the right and you will get your first view of the Window. From this vantage point, it looks impossible that you will actually sit in the Window in about two miles. The steep rock face with the still-tiny opening appears formidable. You can easily see that a fall from the Window would be fatal.

Past the mortars rock, the trail goes through a pretty section. It passes a spring, where there are several small pools of water, and enters a section of ponderosa pine, an indication that you are nearing the highest elevations of the front range of the Catalinas. For a short distance, you are going directly away from the Window, heading west, and you may question whether you are on the correct trail. Then you make a sharp turn and head directly east, toward the Window, switchbacking out of the canyon. About half way up the switchbacks is a signed trail intersection. From here you can join the Finger Rock Trail and go 2.3 miles east to Mount Kimball. The sign indicates that the Flying V Ranch is 5.2 miles away. (This sign is left over from the time when the trail actually began at the Flying V Ranch.) It is now only 1.2 miles on the Ventana Canyon Trail to the Window.

Beyond the sign is a steep, rocky portion of the trail. It crosses the open side of the hill, and it is very easy to lose your way. Watch carefully for cairns. You will want to rest often; fortunately, there are excellent views of the valley. As you come to the top of the switchbacks, you have a pleasant surprise. For about half a mile the trail crosses a saddle and is level. Your legs by this point really don't know how to walk on level ground. After about one-quarter of a mile on the level area, there is a viewpoint to the left of the trail that provides dramatic views of the other side of the mountain. Biosphere II is far off to the right. You can see all of the new development, Sun City Tucson. Forty miles north is Picacho Peak.

The last quarter of a mile climbs steadily to the Window and is a killer, not because it is so terribly steep, but because your legs quickly readjusted to walking on level ground, and, after six miles of climbing, you're tired. When you reach the base of a large rock outcropping, you are almost there. Climb carefully over rocks along the base of the cliff and, suddenly, you are looking at the back of the Window. An orange metal register box placed there by the Southern Arizona Hiking Club contains comments of others who have made the climb. Before you leave, add your own.

I cannot emphasize enough the danger of climbing carelessly in the Window. Remember how it looked from the trail? It's at least one hundred feet straight down. There is a safe, flat ledge for eating lunch and looking at the views. You can see the University of Arizona, the west side of Tucson, and the downtown area. The "A" on "A" Mountain is a tiny letter. Baboquivari Peak is visible, and on a very clear day, you can even see the telescopes at the Kitt Peak Observatory.

After your hike, when you are stopped at the traffic light at Glenn and Campbell headed north, look to your right, high in the Catalinas. If the light is just right, you'll see a tiny opening. Now you know what's really there!

*Note to hiker: This was the way to get there when this guide was printed—check in advance to see if these regulations are still correct. The Coronado National Forest Santa Catalina Ranger District is the number to call for current trail access information, 749-8700.

Pima Canyon Trail

General Description
A long hike through a beautiful canyon into one of the
most rugged areas of the Catalina Mountains

Difficulty
Extremely difficult, easy for first 3.2 miles

Best time of year to hike
Early spring, late fall

Length
7.1 miles

Elevation
2900 feet to 7255 feet

Miles to trailhead from Speedway/Campbell intersection
10

Directions to trailhead from Speedway/Campbell intersection
Go north on Campbell to Skyline Road. Turn left on
Skyline. Skyline turns into Ina Road at the curve. Continue
on Ina Road to Christie Drive. Turn right on Christie Drive.
It reaches a dead end at Magee Road. Turn right on
Magee, and you will see the parking area straight ahead.
This area is private land, and parking signs must be obeyed.

The Pima Canyon Trail is one of the most popular trails in the
front range of the Catalinas. It is easily accessible, not too difficult
for the first three miles, and very scenic.

At the end of Magee Road a sign proclaims that this trailhead is
part of the "Adopt a Trail" program sponsored by Tucson Clean and
Beautiful and Golden Eagle Distributors. Mike Jacob, chairman of cor-
porate affairs for Golden Eagle Distributors, is chairman of Tucson Clean
and Beautiful. According to Jacob, groups that adopt a trailhead (or
park) make a commitment to clean up the area at least once a month.
Tucson Clean and Beautiful is a nonprofit foundation that receives
limited funding from the county and city. Most of its support comes from
private companies. Jacob's company provides released work time
for him and his staff, as well as use of company vehicles.

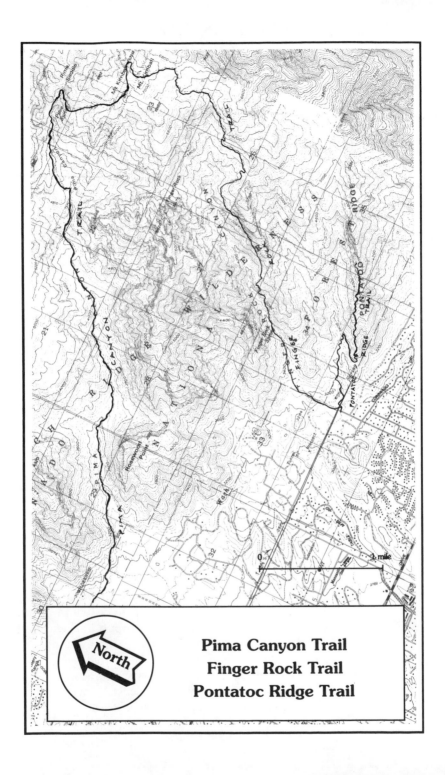

Pima Canyon Trail
Finger Rock Trail
Pontatoc Ridge Trail

North

Pima Canyon Trail

Boy Scout Troop 211 has accepted responsibility for the Pima Canyon trailhead. Troop leader Michael George stated that the boys have a real pride in keeping the area free of debris.

Past the sign and across a few boulders, and you are on a wide trail that leads to an old jeep road. Go left on the road for about twenty feet. A row of small rocks across the road indicates the trail that goes to the right. Despite the rocks, many people continue up the road and have to scramble under a fence to reach the trail. Save yourself this trouble by watching carefully for the rocks.

The well-used trail bears left toward the mountains. This half-mile section crosses private land. Should the owners deny access to this trailhead, the Forest Service has plans to construct another trailhead on national forest land, but until that time, access will continue to be from Magee Road.

You can't miss the entrance to the Coronado National Forest. There is a fence, a walk-through gate, and enough signs for a street intersection. The first sign explains that you are entering a bighorn sheep management area and that dogs must be on a leash. (Dogs are not permitted at all past the Pima Canyon Dam three miles ahead.) A smaller sign indicates that you are entering a National

Forest Wilderness Area that is closed to motor vehicles and motorized equipment. This area is part of the 56,933-acre Pusch Ridge Wilderness Area, which was established in 1978 under the Endangered American Wilderness Act. This designation has been further defined to exclude mountain bikes. Last in line is the actual Pima Canyon Trail sign. An arrow points north to Mount Kimball, which, seven miles ahead, is the final destination of the Pima Canyon Trail.

Past the signs the trail climbs gradually for a few hundred yards before leveling off and heading toward the mountains. The vegetation is typical of the twenty-five hundred- to thirty-two hundred-foot elevations of the Sonora Desert: saguaro, prickly pear, barrel, and cholla cactus; catclaw; ocotillo; brittlebush; mesquite; and palo verde. The views of Tucson from this section show the entire valley. To the south, the 9,453-foot peak of Mount Wrightson is clearly visible, as is the "A" on A Mountain. Far to the west, Baboquivari Peak, sacred mountain of the Tohono O'odham Indians, and the Kitt Peak National Observatory are the dominant landmarks.

After about a mile of easy hiking with some brief climbing, the trail drops sharply into the creek bed. At the creek there is a sign that is not an official Forest Service sign and is misleading. Arrows point to Ina and Magee roads. The distance to Magee Road is indicated as being 2.5 miles. At this point you have hiked a little over a mile, not 2.5 miles, although that may be the mileage down to Ina Road. The only value of the sign is to prevent returning hikers from inadvertently missing the turn to Magee Road.

The creek is dry much of the year, but it is lovely when it is flowing, mostly in winter and spring. The stream bed is wide, and there is a large fire ring in the sandy bottom. Because the danger of flash flooding is very real in these mountains, one should never camp too near, much less *in* a stream bottom.

As you cross the creek and round a curve, the city disappears. This is one of the joys of living in Tucson and having the Catalinas in your backyard. Within an hour of hiking, you can escape the city. The trail parallels the stream for the next two miles, occasionally crossing to the other side. Even when the stream is running, it is easy to boulder-hop across. A half mile into the canyon and the first cottonwoods appear. Soon the giant trees provide a canopy, and you are walking in the shade. This is one of the prettiest areas on the lower portion of the Pima Canyon Trail.

Unfortunately, not everyone who comes to Pima Canyon treats it with respect. I was dismayed by the careless building of fire rings—one large one right in the middle of the trail—and the failure to remove debris from the fire pits. The code of the wilderness, "Take only pictures, leave only footprints," is foreign to many who hike the first part of the Pima Canyon Trail. Perhaps it is too close to the city and too easy.

As you leave the dense trees, the canyon opens up. The drainage from Pusch Ridge comes in from the north. Pusch Ridge is the prime habitat of the bighorn sheep, and, if you're lucky, you may spot one of these magnificent creatures standing on a rock outcropping.

Here the trail becomes confusing, crossing the narrow stream bed several times. If you are in doubt as to the correct route of the trail, stop, look for cairns indicating direction, or rows of rocks blocking the wrong way. The ascent to the canyon becomes slightly more difficult. After a particularly steep, but mercifully short, climb, you'll know you are nearing the Pima Canyon Dam. You will cross several large slabs of rock right before the dam.

Shortly a metal sign indicates that you have reached the point in the bighorn sheep management area that is closed to dogs. A few yards ahead and to the left of the sign is the Pima Canyon Dam, built by the Arizona Game and Fish Division as a source of water for wildlife. This is a good lunch spot. Secluded in a bend of the canyon, you would never know that a city of 700,000 was only three miles away. Flowers cling to the drainage around the dam. Birds chatter and occasionally dive down for a drink. It is no wonder that in an earlier time, around A.D. 1000, this spot was home to the Hohokam Indians. Two hundred yards to the left of the dam as you face down the canyon are bedrock mortars, depressions in the rock formed by Indian women grinding mesquite beans. Two mortars are very deep, and there are several smaller ones nearby. It is easy to imagine Indian women sitting on the rocks, chatting and grinding beans while their men hunted.

It takes the average hiker about two hours to reach this point. You have hiked three miles and gained approximately eight hundred feet in elevation, from twenty-nine hundred feet at the trailhead to thirty-seven hundred feet at the dam. This first portion of the trail is a good introduction to the canyons of the Catalinas and is a good turnaround spot for a beginning hiker.

A lot more is ahead if you choose to continue up the canyon.
For another mile the elevation gain is gradual. The saguaro disappear and are replaced by a few scrub oak and Mexican blue oak.
The trail crosses one of the loveliest spots in Pima Canyon. Huge
slabs of rock interspersed with pools of water make another
excellent picnic site. To the right is a dam, this one larger than the
first one.

Beyond this dam, the trail begins to climb sharply. You are
headed into one of the most rugged sections of the Catalinas—and
one of the most dramatically beautiful.

You climb continually for another mile, until you reach Pima
Canyon Spring. At the spring you will have come 5.2 miles from
the trailhead and gained 2,550 feet. This spring provides a permanent source of water. As you approach the spring, there are two
concrete tanks, which, as you will see shortly, are connected by
pipe to a spring above.

Again, careless hikers have spoiled an otherwise beautiful area.
When I last hiked this trail I found a metal garbage can by the
tanks, upset, and waiting, probably forever, for the garbage col-
lector. A large blue foam rubber mat is thrown beside the can. The
pipe connecting the tanks with the spring is broken, so there is no
water in the tanks. At the spring there is an enclosed structure with
a broken door leaning against the opening. Beyond the door is the
actual spring.

There are several good campsites around the spring area, also
spoiled with debris. My hiking companion and I nearly filled a
garbage bag with refuse from the area. A Safeway plastic grocery
bag, a three-pound coffee can, a sandwich bag, an empty raisin
box, and the bottom half of a pair of pants that must have gotten
too hot were some of the items that we carried out of the spring
area. If you can overlook unnecessary fire rings and the trash, it is a
beautiful spot, surrounded by oak and a few ponderosa pine.

Above the spring you have to be a serious, well-conditioned
hiker to continue. Study the map carefully, and you will get an indication of what is ahead. Mount Kimball is at seventy-two hundred
feet; you are at 5,550 feet. It is a rough two miles to the summit.

As you leave the canyon from the spring, you climb sharply
along an open hillside. The views of the city to the south, and of
the canyon to the north, are awesome. Looking up the canyon,
actually climbing it doesn't appear possible.

A half mile into the climb and you come to a small sign pointing to Pima Saddle. A short spur trail leads to the saddle, and if you have time the views are worth it. You get a glimpse of the "other side of the mountain." From this sign to Mount Kimball is some of the most difficult climbing and trail finding in the Catalinas. As my hiking companion said, "There are a hundred places you can break your leg" and "This is the worst trail I have ever been on!" The general plan is to climb around the west side of Mount Kimball to the high ridge that connects Mount Kimball and Finger Rock.

Despite the difficulty, in terms of scenery and views, the trip up the canyon and to Mount Kimball is, for want of a better word, spectacular. How many people can say they have seen the back of Finger Rock? As you near Mount Kimball, the ponderosa pines tower above you. As you near the top, a small sign points the way to Mount Kimball, and soon you will have reached your goal, climbing seven miles and gaining 4,355 feet in elevation. You feel like you are on top of the world. Look north and you see Biosphere II near Oracle. To the east is Mount Lemmon; to the south, all of Tucson.

The trip up and down the Pima Canyon Trail requires the entire day. Depending on your conditioning, I would estimate at least six hours up and five hours back, allowing reasonable time for resting and enjoying the views from the top. An interesting variation is to come up the Pima Canyon Trail and descend by way of the shorter Finger Rock Trail. This requires leaving a vehicle at each trailhead, but it will shorten the return trip.

The Pima Canyon Trail is one of the most beautiful of the trails in the front range of the Catalinas; unfortunately, as we have seen, it is one of the most mistreated. Whatever portion of this trail you decide to hike, don't leave any evidence that you have been there.

Finger Rock Trail

General Description

A steep climb through a beautiful canyon, with spectacular views from the high point, Mount Kimball

Difficulty

Extremely difficult, steep, continuous climbing after the first mile

Best time of year to hike

Spring, fall

Length

5 miles

Elevation

3100 feet at trailhead; 7255 feet on Mount Kimball

Miles to trailhead from Speedway/Campbell intersection

8.4

Directions to trailhead from Speedway/Campbell intersection

Go north on Campbell Avenue 6.2 miles to Skyline Drive. Turn right on Skyline Drive for .5 miles. At this point Skyline divides and turns left. Continue on Skyline for .7 miles to the intersection with Alvernon Way. Turn left on Alvernon Way, which reaches a dead end at the trailhead after 1 mile.

A dominant landmark of the Catalinas is Finger Rock, a tall rock spire that points skyward about midway through the range. It is possible to get a better view of that rock spire by climbing the Finger Rock Trail to Mount Kimball through some of the most spectacular scenery in the Catalinas.

The well-marked trail begins at the end of the road to the left of a sign indicating that this is a bighorn sheep management area and that dogs must be on a leash and are not permitted at all past Finger Rock Spring.

The trail heads into Finger Rock Canyon through an impressive stand of saguaros and is basically level until the spring. The spring, a permanent water source, empties into a partially covered concrete tank to the left of the trail. Some effort has been made to clean the

Finger Rock Formation

area, and there is a lot of dead foliage, including a large cottonwood tree. Do not follow the trail that continues level beyond the
spring unless you want to spend some time in the canyon bottom.
The Finger Rock Trail switchbacks to the right, up the side of the
canyon. As you work your way up the switchbacks, Finger Rock
appears larger; however, this is as close as the trail comes to the
actual rock formation.

After the switchbacks, the trail drops into a small drainage. This
section has many amoles (nicknamed shindaggers), and it is important to stay on the trail to avoid being punctured in the shins by the
sharp spines of the plant. The trail continues to climb around the
canyon basin. There are no parts of the Finger Rock Trail that could
be termed easy. In fact, except for a few very short sections, the
Finger Rock Trail is relentless in its climb to Mount Kimball. The
views are excellent, however, and always worth the climb.

After about two miles you reach a large, flat rock, which is a
good resting spot. You have gained enough elevation that the
saguaros have disappeared and have been replaced by piñon pine,
juniper, and scrub oak. Finger Rock is now obscured by the cliffs
and will not be visible for the remainder of the hike.

There are some places in this portion that can be confusing. There is a side trail to the right that leads to an overlook called Linda Vista Saddle, but it involves some very steep, unnecessary climbing. Wait a few hundred yards for a second trail to the right, which will get you to the saddle with very little effort.

Before reaching this second trail to the right, you will see a distinct trail to the left. Even though this trail is blocked by a row of small rocks, it looks like the logical trail to take to Mount Kimball, and many hikers mistakenly head in this direction. Don't! Continue on the main trail, which bears to the right. On this main trail and immediately after a short, steep section, a spur trail goes to the right and is the correct route to reach Linda Vista Saddle. The spur trail is level except for a brief climb at the end.

Linda vista means "beautiful view," and that's exactly what the area provides. From the saddle you can see the entire Tucson Valley. Westin La Paloma Resort looks like a pink dollhouse below. This is a good turnaround spot if you want a short hike. It takes about two and one-half hours to hike the three miles to the saddle.

If you choose to continue the remaining two miles to Mount Kimball, expect some steep climbing ahead. Take the spur trail from Linda Vista Saddle back to the main trail and continue around the basin. Scrub oak shades the trail, and you pass beneath huge boulders. Mistletoe hangs from most of the trees. For a short period the trail is smooth, but it soon becomes rocky again. Baboquivari Peak, Kitt Peak, and most of the west side of the city, including downtown Tucson and the white buildings of the Arizona Health Sciences Center, are visible from here.

The scenery in this section is dramatic, with stark cliffs towering above the tall ponderosas. The carpet of soft pine needles is quite a treat after the rocky trail. There are several excellent camping spots and two small drainages that are likely to hold water during winter and early spring.

Past the pines, you come to a more open area, covered with manzanita and small scrub oaks. The city spreads out below, and the views are great. Unfortunately, pine needles yield to rocks again.

As you begin to top out, you come to a large rock cairn on the left of the trail. There is no sign, but this is the spot where you turn left to make the final half-mile climb to Mount Kimball. If you miss the cairn, you will be on the way to the Window, so look for it carefully.

Past the cairn the trail turns north and once again begins to climb through piñon pine and juniper. Soon you are hiking under the ponderosas, and this is a lovely portion of the hike. A short, steep climb across a slab of rock and you come to a sign on a tree indicating that Pima Canyon is to the left and Mount Kimball straight ahead.

Follow the trail along the crest for about two hundred yards and you will come to a large, flat rock outcropping that is an excellent lunch spot and lookout. Depending on your conditioning, it will take four to five hours to reach Mount Kimball, and almost as long to return.

To use an old hiking cliche, the views are worth every step. The Finger Rock Trail takes you to the heart of the Catalinas. Cathedral Rock and Mount Lemmon are to the east. West you can see part of Pusch Ridge. Northwest is Picacho Peak, Sun City Tucson and, almost due north, the white structures of Biosphere II.

Most who hike to the summit of Mount Kimball would be surprised to learn that the peak was named for an early developer, Frederick E. A. Kimball. Kimball moved to Tucson in 1899 and lived here until his death in 1930. He was one of the first property owners in Summerhaven, and, during the summers, served as postmaster of the tiny village. He urged the building of a short road to Mount Lemmon and promoted the development of Summerhaven as a summer recreation area. At the time of his death, Kimball was secretary-treasurer of the Summerhaven Land and Improvement Company.

In addition to his interest in Summerhaven, Kimball owned a printing business and a book and stationery store in Tucson. At one time he was a reporter for the *Arizona Daily Star.* He was elected to the Arizona legislature for four terms, and at the time of his death was serving in the state senate. As senator, Kimball secured passage of the state's first child-welfare bill and supported the establishment of the Catalina Game Preserve.

An ardent outdoorsman, Kimball was a member of the Game Protective Association and an organizer of the Tucson Natural History Society. It was this group that appealed to the United States Geographic Board to name a peak in the Catalinas in his memory. The previously unnamed peak was officially designated Mount Kimball by the USGB on 4 February 1931.

Although Kimball spent much time hiking in the Catalinas in the area around Summerhaven, it is not known whether he ever stood atop the peak that was named after him. It is certain that he would have been pleased with the choice.

Pontatoc Ridge Trail

General Description
> A short, fun hike to the top of a ridge in the front range of the Catalinas

Difficulty
> Moderate, short areas of steep climbing

Best time of year to hike
> Spring, fall, winter

Length
> 2.6 miles

Elevation
> 3100 feet at trailhead; 4400 feet at mine entrance

Miles to trailhead from Speedway/Campbell intersection
> 8.4

Directions to trailhead from Speedway/Campbell intersection
> Go north on Campbell Avenue 6.2 miles to Skyline Drive. Turn right on Skyline Drive for .5 miles. At this point Skyline divides and turns left. Continue on Skyline for .7 miles to the intersection with Alvernon Way. Turn left on Alvernon Way, which reaches a dead end at the trailhead after 1 mile.

The Pontatoc Ridge and Canyon trails are named after the old Pontotoc Mine, now buried in someone's backyard in Coronado Foothills Estates. This very un-Southwestern name comes from a Chickasaw Indian word, "pakitakohlih," which means "hanging grapes." Pakitakohlih was a Chickasaw village in the 1540s when DeSoto explored the Mississippi River. The name was corrupted through the years and by the late 1700s was called "Pontotoc." When Mississippi became a state, the Chickasaw were relocated to the Indian Territory of Oklahoma, where they named their new town "Pontotoc."

The mystery is—how did the name of a Chickasaw Indian village become the name of a mine in Tucson? There is no record of the mine at the Pima County Recorder's Office. For many years the road to the mine was called Pontotoc Road and on early maps

Pontatoc Ridge Trail

was spelled "Pontotoc." By the early 1950s, the maps showed "Pontatoc," a spelling error that entered officialdom when the area around the mine site was made into the Coronado Foothills Estate in 1961. This error was continued on maps of the Santa Catalina Mountains.

There are no signs marking the beginning of the Pontatoc Ridge and Canyon trails. The joint trailhead starts on the right side of the parking area, immediately beyond three short telephone poles that block an old jeep road. The road narrows quickly into the trail, which is the starting point for the ascent of both the ridge and the canyon.

As you begin, look to the northeast. A stark triangular ridge with what appears to be several caves in the cliff dominates the skyline. This is Pontatoc Ridge. The Pontatoc Ridge Trail ends to the right of the largest opening in the cliff, which is actually an abandoned mine.

In recent years the area near the trailhead has become a favorite teenage hangout. There are many side trails leading to fire rings, making the first .8 miles of the trail confusing. The following description is purposely detailed. Follow it carefully, and you will be rewarded with a great little hike that provides dramatic views of Tucson. In addition, you'll get a better understanding of the early mining history of the Catalinas.

You may feel like a mouse wandering through a maze in search of cheese on the lower section of this trail! Several false trails lead off to the right and are tempting to take because they appear to head directly for the ridge, but remember to keep bearing slightly to the left, heading for the cliff. To further confuse you, after about half a mile, there is a distinct trail to the left that is deceptive. It is blocked by a small row of rocks, so be careful to avoid this side trail, as it reaches a dead end at the top of a hill.

After about .6 miles, the trail drops into a small drainage, comes out, and descends into another, somewhat deeper drainage. Shortly you come to a third drainage, which is deep and very pronounced. This is the lower part of Pontatoc Canyon. If there has been adequate rainfall, there may be water running. At any time of year there is an assortment of wildflowers, making this a pretty spot.

It is a steep climb out of the drainage, and you enter an area that is covered with amoles (shindaggers), those spearlike plants that attack you at shin level. The vegetation is mostly palo verde and mesquite trees; prickly pear, cholla, and barrel cacti; and ocotillos. There is no thick stand of saguaros on this trail, unlike most of the trails of the front range.

As you go up the switchbacks, begin to look carefully for a trail that leads off to the right. There is a large cairn at the intersection, but it may not be there when you attempt the hike. The trail is distinct and cannot be missed. The turnoff is at .8 miles and goes at a right angle to the main trail, which continues up Pontatoc Canyon. You will be taking the Ridge Trail, which quickly levels off along the side of the ridge. This is a pleasant part of the trail, with excellent views of the west side of Tucson and Finger Rock. As you round the ridge, the entire city spreads out below.

There is a large, flat rocky area that is good for lunch or just relaxing. If you are careful, this spot is excellent for a hike during a full moon. A perfect scenario is to hike up right before sunset, watch the sun go down, the moon rise, and the lights of the city come on as you enjoy a picnic dinner!

For about half a mile the trail is again hard to follow. There are cairns that mark the general direction, but, should they be gone, remember to bear to the left slightly and continue up the ridge.

There are several steep step-ups. One section looks like someone deliberately planted teddy bear cholla and, for about one-quarter of a mile, you have to be very careful not to bump into one, or you will learn why they are called "jumping" cactus.

Beyond the cholla, for about half a mile, the trail is a slab of rock, and it is easy to stray. You want to go to the left of the large rock outcropping. Watch carefully for rows of rocks blocking the trail. There are times when it appears that you should go to the right, when most of the time the trail is actually to the left. If you do get off the trail, it is not disastrous, and you will wander back on the correct path.

You continue to climb gradually for about three-quarters of a mile, occasionally encountering a few minor switchbacks, including one set that goes to the right. When the trail levels off, look to the right and you will see a large hole that at one time must have been a prospector's pit, or as the miners would say, a "gopher hole." Right past the partially filled hole is what looks like a scooped-out trough in the rock. It could be a natural formation, but it looks man-made. The scooped-out area makes a good lookout point for views of Pontatoc Canyon and Finger Rock. Below, you can see where the Pontatoc Canyon Trail switchbacks out of the canyon.

From this point the Pontatoc Ridge Trail is distinct, as it makes its way to the mine area. Very shortly you come to a saddle. To the right of the trail are excellent views of the east side of Tucson. You look down on the Skyline Country Club and the homes of the Skyline Country Club Estates.

Past the saddle the trail becomes steeper and is quite rocky. As you get closer to the ridge, there is more evidence of mining activity, and the openings in the cliff are clearly visible. The trail ends near a mine entrance, which is open for about two hundred yards. These open mines can be dangerous and should not be entered.

Open mines are one of the dangers of hiking in the Catalinas. According to Bill Lewis, minerals and land staff specialist of the Santa Catalina District of the Coronado National Forest, the Forest Service does not close all the dangerous shafts in the mountains for several reasons. First, there are hundreds of such shafts, making the job a complicated and expensive one. In addition, he explained, "Bats have begun to use the shafts, and obstructing the entrance may wipe out a species of bats. Before we could close the entrance, a study would have to be made of the bat population." He further explained that there may be items of historical significance in the mine that also would have to be studied. What the Forest Service has done occasionally is to build a fence around the entrance, but this requires annual maintenance, and the Forest Service is already short-staffed.

Be content to stay away from the open mine tunnel and enjoy the views of the canyon and the city. I'm sure the miners who worked these mines in 1917 and 1918 didn't view this area as a place to come for fun! All the work done on this ridge was done by hand, and the ore carried out on the backs of mules. The miners would have enjoyed the luxury of sitting and looking at the views of the city.

Pusch Peak Trail

General Description

> A difficult hike to the high point of the western end of the Catalinas that offers panoramic 360-degree views

Difficulty

> Extremely difficult, all steep climbing, rock scrambling

Best time of year to hike

> Spring, fall, moderate winter days

Length

> 2.5 miles

Elevation

> 2650 feet at the trailhead; 5361 feet at Pusch Peak

Miles to trailhead from Speedway/Campbell intersection

> 12.8

Directions to trailhead from Speedway/Campbell intersection

> Go north on Campbell Avenue to Skyline. Turn left on Skyline. Skyline becomes Ina Road at the curve. Continue on Ina Road to Oracle Road and turn right. Follow Oracle Road north 3.1 miles to the intersection with Linda Vista Road. Turn right on Linda Vista Road. The parking area for the trailhead is .2 miles on Linda Vista Road and is on the right.

Pusch Peak was named for George Pusch, an early Tucson rancher and businessman. Pusch came to the United States from Germany in 1865. He settled in New York, working as an apprentice butcher. Enamored with the idea of being a cowboy, Pusch spent a month's wages on a pair of red cowboy boots and headed for California, where he planned to become a cattleman, "Py Gott" (his favorite expression).

He worked at odd jobs until 1874, when he purchased a team of mules and crossed the desert to Tucson to join his boyhood friend, John Zellweger. Pusch and Zellweger pooled their resources and bought a ranch near Canada del Oro, fourteen miles north of Tucson. They registered their PZ brand and installed a steam pump. The ranch became known as the Steam Pump Ranch.

Pusch and Zellweger opened a butcher shop in Tucson in 1875.

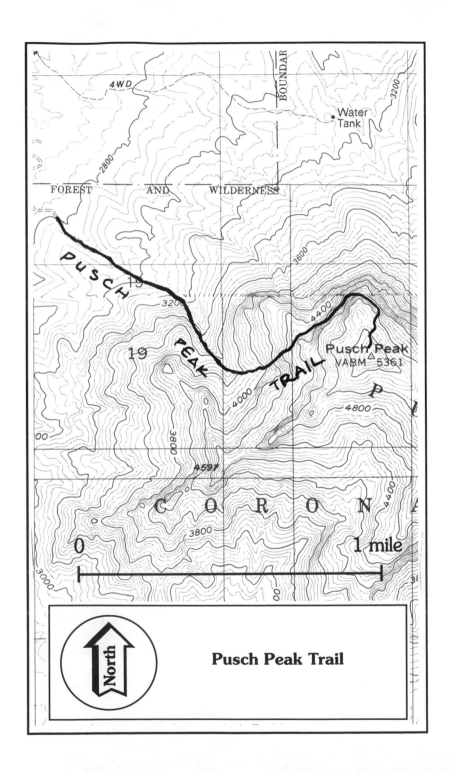

Pusch Peak Trail

Hiker going down steep ridge near summit, Pusch Peak Trail

As their business grew, they purchased other ranches, until the two owned nearly fifteen thousand range cattle.

Although he was a good businessman and a shrewd judge of cattle, Pusch never reached his goal of being a real cowboy. Once, while helping drive fifteen hundred steers to the San Carlos Indian Reservation, a wild steer chased him. As he ran for the corral, his belt came loose, his pants fell down, and he fell flat on his face. A cowboy shot the steer, saving Pusch's life. As Pusch got to his feet, he exclaimed, "Py Gott, dot vas close."

The route to Pusch Ridge is not an official trail and, therefore, is not maintained by the Forest Service. Originally constructed by a Boy Scout troop, it has through constant use become a fairly well-defined route to the top. The summit of Pusch Peak provides spectacular views of Tucson and, although extremely difficult to reach, is worth the effort required. An added enticement for hiking this trail is the chance to see one of the desert bighorn sheep that inhabit this area.

The trail begins through a gate to the right of the parking area. A bridle trail leads off to the right. The route to Pusch Peak is the one to the left. At first a narrow trail, it quickly joins an old jeep

road and climbs gradually toward the mountains. After approximately .3 miles a side trail leads to the right. You should continue
to the left. As you climb you come to a hitching rail and a barbeque
grill used by the Sheraton El Conquistador Resort for cookouts. (As
a side note, there are several bridle trails in this area that can
confuse the hiker. If the trail shows evidence of heavy use by
horses, it is usually not the segment of the trail that you should use.)

Past the picnic area, the trail parallels the drainage and changes
from a wide jeep road to a narrow trail. There is a magnificent
stand of large, healthy saguaros as you approach the base of the
mountains.

In this section there are several trail forks, and it is important to
heed the following directions carefully. At the first fork past the
picnic area, a trail leads to the left. Don't go on this trail. Walk a
few steps and then turn left where a second trail forks. The trail
crosses a small drainage and quickly reaches another trail fork. This
time, turn right and toward a major drainage.

As you progress into the drainage, you can see what is, in
times of heavy rainfall or snowmelt, a large waterfall. Most of the
year there is some water trickling over the rocks. Many side trails
lead down into the drainage. In fact, the original route of the trail
crossed the drainage and climbed to the east side of the waterfall,
then recrossed the drainage to the west side. Although it is still possible to follow this route, I prefer to remain on the trail that climbs
the west (or right) side of this drainage.

In the first of many steep climbs, the trail climbs sharply to the
right, away from the drainage, to an outcropping of rocks high
above the waterfall. From this vantage point, you look down on the
waterfall. A dam built by the Arizona Game and Fish Department
backs up a small pond that provides a permanent source of water
for wildlife. This is apparently a popular camping area and, unfortunately, usually marred by the trash and even the orange spray paint
of the users.

The trail climbs high above the west side of the drainage and is
relatively easy to follow from this point on. There is another small
dam a short distance up the drainage. There are places where the
trail splits, but it always returns to a main trail. Many cairns have
been placed along the trail. You cannot go wrong if you stay on the
west side of the drainage and steadily climb. It is not until you reach
the very head of the drainage that the trail drops briefly into the

now small and narrow drainage, crossing between two trees to the
other side.

After crossing the drainage, the trail heads directly for the base
of a solid band of cliffs. The cliffs are your goal for nearly a mile.
From this point until the summit, the trail is extremely rugged. Any
climbing that preceded this point could be considered moderate! It is
what I call an "all fours" (or coming back, a "sit and slide") trail!
Seriously, the trail is treacherous, and it is foolish to take unnecessary chances.

The saving grace of this climb is the view of the northwest
valley. Forty miles north is the stark triangular outline of Picacho
Peak. To the northeast are the white domed structures of Biosphere
II. Spread out to the northwest are the checkerboard farms of
Marana. Right below is the luxury resort, the Sheraton El Conquistador, whose guests would be amazed to know that you are
actually climbing that mountain.

As you reach the base of the cliffs, the trail rounds the cliffs
and comes to an area that appears to be the summit; but, as with
so many trails, the summit is just a little farther—a quarter mile up
the trail. As you reach the summit, the other side of the Catalinas
becomes visible, and finally, on the summit, you can see all of the
Tucson Valley. As George Pusch would say, "Py Gott!"

Depending on your hiking conditioning, the summit can be
reached in three to four hours. The return trip takes less, usually
about two hours.

The U.S. Geological Survey vertical altitude benchmark is in
one of the rocks on the summit. A large triangular metal tower used
at one time to test the number of lightning strikes on Pusch Peak
has fallen over and now provides a surface on which many hikers
leave their names or initials.

The 360-degree view from the summit of Pusch Peak is one of
the best in the Catalina Mountains. The climb to the summit
requires stamina and persistence, but it is one that should be made
at least once by everyone who enjoys the Catalinas.

Romero Canyon Trail

General Description
A hike to a canyon with deep year-round pools suitable for swimming

Difficulty
Moderate, some areas of steep climbing

Best time of year to hike
Spring, fall, winter

Length
2.8 miles

Elevation
2700 feet at trailhead; 3700 feet at Romero pools

Miles to trailhead from Speedway/Campbell intersection
15.7

Directions to trailhead from Speedway/Campbell intersection
Go north on Campbell Avenue to Skyline Drive. Turn left on Skyline Drive. Skyline becomes Ina Road at the curve. Continue on Ina Road to Oracle Road. Turn right on Oracle and continue north 6.2 miles to the entrance to Catalina State Park. There is a $3 per vehicle entry charge to enter the park. Drive to the trailhead parking area at the end of the road. The Romero Canyon trailhead is to the right, past the bulletin board and restrooms.

Romero Canyon is a spectacular canyon on the north side of the Santa Catalina Mountains. The Romero Canyon Trail leads into the mountains and connects with the west fork of Sabino Trail, enabling the adventurous hiker to cross the mountains into Sabino Canyon, or, by intersecting with the Mount Lemmon Trail, to climb the summit of Mount Lemmon. This trail description is for the first 2.8 miles of the Romero Canyon Trail, the portion that leads to an area known as Romero Pools.

The pools and canyon are named after Fabian Romero, who in 1889 established Rancho Romero in Canada del Oro, near where Oracle Junction is today. The ranch, the first in that area, covered forty-eight hundred acres.

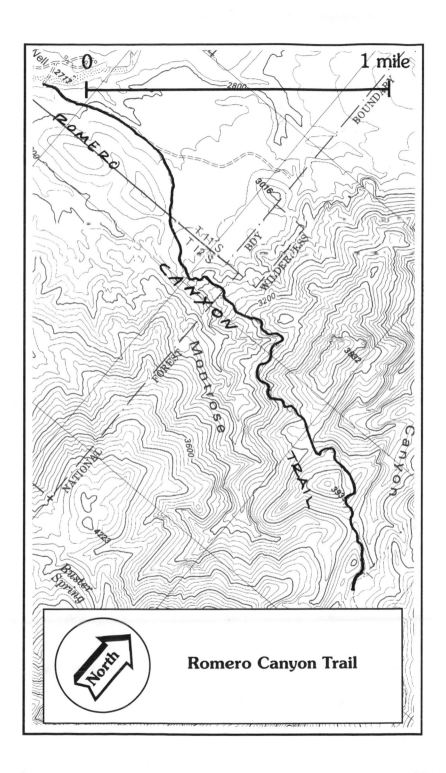

Romero Canyon Trail

One of the pools in Romero Canyon, Romero Canyon Trail

The trail into this lush canyon begins right beyond the restrooms and immediately crosses Sutherland Wash. If there has been adequate rainfall or snowmelt, the wash will be running, and you must boulder hop or wade across. Once across the wash the trail climbs immediately to the east. Railroad ties across the trail prevent erosion but require stepping up steeply at times. At the top of the first rise is a level area where the park rangers have placed two benches, making a good spot to sit, rest, and view the scene below.

The trail continues southeast to the intersection of the Canyon Loop Trail and the Romero Trail. The Canyon Loop Trail is a pleasant two and one-half mile loop that connects with the Sutherland Trail to return to the parking area. The Romero Trail continues straight ahead, level and sandy, and wide enough to be a road. It passes through a large stand of mesquite and heads directly for the base of the mountains. After one-quarter of a mile, another intersection is reached, with the Romero and Montrose Canyon trails. Montrose Canyon is a deep canyon to the west, with several large pools. A steep trail leads down into the canyon. The trail is not maintained, and a sign warns Danger—Unsafe Footing Beyond this Point.

The Romero Canyon Trail climbs to the left of the intersection and immediately becomes narrow and rocky. At the National Forest Boundary sign, hikers are warned that dogs are not permitted beyond this point. The trail climbs steadily, and the views of both the valley and the mountains are excellent. This is a heavily used trail, and many hikers have made side trails leading to lookout points, which may temporarily cause you to stray off the trail. Also, the trail occasionally splits, but it always returns to the main trail, making whichever direction you take all right. For the most part, the trail is clearly marked, and there is no question as to the route.

The trail circles the drainage, gradually climbing toward the crest of the ridge. The vegetation is diverse in the shelter of the drainage. Small saguaros are thriving under their "nurse" trees. In spring the wildflowers are profuse. The entire area is a jumble of boulders.

As the trail continues to climb, it goes through a slit in the rock and then seriously begins climbing toward the crest of the ridge. A series of steep, rocky switchbacks brings you to the top of the ridge. There are several places where the trail has been "shortcut," a hiking term meaning that hikers have cut across a switchback, going straight up to the trail rather than using the switchback. Shortcutting causes erosion and is not good hiking etiquette. Unfortunately, any trail that is used by a great number of people attracts many who are not concerned about the effects of their actions on the environment. In a few years this section of the trail will be seriously eroded unless preventive maintenance is done.

The views of the Catalinas from the ridge are spectacular in this area, and you realize that you are entering rugged country. From the crest of this first ridge, the trail descends briefly and crosses a saddle between two ridges. To the left, after about .2 miles, you get your first view of Romero Canyon. There is a large waterfall at the base of the canyon. It appears as if it is possible to climb down to the waterfall from this point, but the route is treacherous, and it is better to work your way down farther along the trail and nearer the creek. Fortunately the trail does not climb the steep ridge in front of you but circles it to the northeast. This portion of the trail, shaded by scrub oak, is especially beautiful, with the views of the canyon on the left. As the trail drops into Romero Canyon, you can see the area called Romero Pools. It takes the average hiker two to two and one-half hours to reach the pool area. The trail crosses the stream, and from there it is possible to boulder hop to the several pools that continue downstream.

At one large pool, a diving rope has been attached to a tree. The pools are deep and in summer, especially, make an inviting scene. The lush vegetation and the water creates a little paradise. Unfortunately there seems to be a correlation between the accessibility of an area and the amount of trash left by careless campers. What could be an incredibly beautiful area is marred by trash and too many fire rings. Nevertheless, it is worth the hike to see the rugged beauty of Romero Pools.

Butterfly Trail Loop

General Description
A beautiful high-elevation hike through thick pine forests and past a permanent spring

Difficulty
Moderate

Best time of year to hike
Summer, spring, fall

Length
5.7 miles from Soldier Camp to Palisades Ranger Station

Elevation
7700 feet at Soldier Camp; 6700 feet at Novio Spring; 7950 feet at Palisades Ranger Station

Miles to trailhead from Speedway/Campbell intersection
33.8

Directions to trailhead from Speedway/Campbell intersection
This hike is best done using a two-car shuttle. Drive east on Speedway Boulevard to Wilmot Road. Turn left on Wilmot Road. Wilmot Road turns into Tanque Verde Road at Pima. Continue on Tanque Verde Road to the Catalina Highway. Turn left on Catalina Highway to Mount Lemmon. Follow the Catalina Highway up the mountain to the Palisades Ranger Station. Leave one car at the Ranger Station and drive 2.9 miles farther to a parking area on the right by Soldier Camp Road. The Butterfly Trail trailhead is at this parking area.

On 25 July 1935, one thousand acres were set aside near Butterfly Peak to preserve one of the most varied areas of vegetation in the Southwest. Ranging in elevation from eighty-three hundred feet near Kellogg Mountain to sixty-seven hundred feet at Novio Spring, the Butterfly Trail Loop is a classroom for the botanist and the hiker.

The Butterfly Trail begins as an old jeep road. In two hundred yards the road forks. Take the fork to the left. The road reaches a dead end and becomes a trail. The correct trail is on the left side of the end of the road.

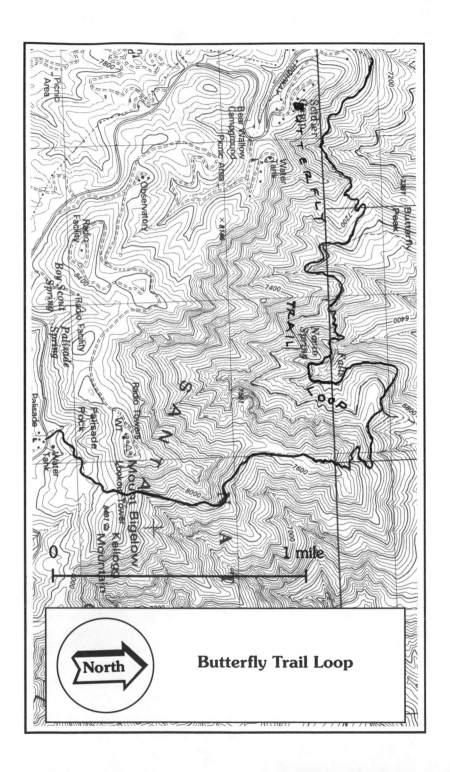

Butterfly Trail Loop

Dense pine forests make the Butterfly Trail Loop an excellent summer hike

The trail begins as a long, gradual slope down the north side of the ridge, through thick forests of ponderosa pine and fir. Through the trees you can catch a glimpse of the large mine complex at San Manuel, including two smokestacks and a large tailings pond.

The trail circles the basin to the point of a ridge, where a rocky outcropping makes a good stopping spot. From this outcropping the trail turns to the right and switchbacks steeply down the mountain. After about a mile, a faint trail leads to Butterfly Peak, .4 miles ahead. The Butterfly Trail continues to switchback to the right and quickly comes to an open area with few trees. The hillside here is covered with large ferns. You soon return to the magnificent, huge ponderosa pines. The cool shade and green vegetation is welcome in summer, when Tucson temperatures are normally at least one hundred degrees.

At 1.4 miles there is a signed trail intersection. Continue on the trail to the right, following the arrow to Bigelow I.O. There is a slight uphill trek before the trail levels off and drops into a ravine. Water trickles in this ravine for most of the year. These ravines are beautiful areas. Usually devoid of trees, they are covered with flowers. In early summer, butterflies hover around the plants, probably the reason for the name of the peak and the trail. After climbing out of the ravine, the trail winds along the side of the hill for a quarter of a mile before dropping into a larger ravine.

After climbing out of this ravine, the trail again goes around the hill, through pine and fir. After a quarter of a mile, the trail again begins to switchback steeply down the hill, and it becomes rocky for a time. It soon emerges on an open ridge. The television towers are visible to the southwest. Views of the mine from this point are excellent. You are looking down into Alder Canyon. The switchbacks leading down into the canyon are very steep. The east side of the canyon is exposed, with the vegetation being mostly scrub oak. As you approach the bottom, the trees reappear, this time pines and some large alders and oaks.

As you drop down into the head of the canyon, there is a huge boulder on the right. From this point on, most of your route will be uphill until a slight down grade into the Palisades Ranger Station. About fifty yards past the huge rock, you begin to see large shelves of rock on the left. At the base of the rocks are small pools of water. If the runoff is enough, there will be a falls in this area. This area is known as Novio Spring. The trail goes along the creek through a spectacular section. There are large ferns, flowers, and small pools of water. Butterflies and hummingbirds flitter about the flowers. Across the creek is a nice campsite. The trail continues to parallel the creek past the campsite. Here the trail is easy to lose. It crosses a pile of rocks and then crosses a fork of the creek to the left and begins to climb out of the canyon. For a short distance the trail goes along the left side of the creek, where again there are usually some small pools.

The trail switchbacks steeply out of the canyon and away from the creek. There is a short section of scrub oak that quickly gives way to fir trees. There are a few trees that have an unusual feature. So much debris from falling leaves has been caught in the lower branches of these trees that other trees have taken seed and are actually growing in them.

One of the most interesting things about this trail is the changing vegetation. About half a mile past the creek there is an area of really mixed vegetation. This is at about six thousand feet. There are fir, ponderosa pine, oak, and locust trees. It is like nature wasn't exactly sure what belonged there—or conditions are right for a variety of trees. As the trail climbs the side of the hill, it comes to an open section with mostly scrub oak. The views of Alder Canyon are good, and you can appreciate the vastness of the area you are hiking.

There are quite a few yucca plants, Mexican thistles, and even prickly pear and hedgehog cacti. Alligator junipers begin to appear. You quickly come to a saddle, which is a little over half way into the hike. From here the trailhead at Soldier Camp is 3.2 miles. Palisades Ranger Station is 2.5 miles away. A wooden sign marks this intersection, but it should not be relied on to be there when you do this hike. The correct route is to continue ahead across the saddle and slightly to the right.

The trail again changes character and becomes very pleasant and cool. The mine and other side of the mountain is again in view. The vegetation is back to large fir trees. As you look through the trees across the mountain, you can see the old road that goes up Mount Lemmon from Oracle. About midway up the mountain is a large water tank and a small mining operation. Views like this provide an understanding of why the term "islands in the sky" is used to refer to the desert mountains of the southeastern part of Arizona. In the summer it is one hundred degrees in the city below, and here is this cool, green island where the temperatures rarely reach eighty.

From the saddle the trail climbs gradually through a thick pine forest. A small stand of aspen is trying to survive in the midst of the forest; some are huge trees, and others are very small and will probably be choked out. It is an incredibly beautiful area.

The trail climbs out of this section into a small saddle. A trail leads off to the left to several good campsites. The Butterfly Trail continues to the right, switchbacking for a short distance to a rock outcropping with a seat carved out especially for you—or so it seems. From this seat the line of the San Pedro River is visible as a line of green.

Past this rock the trail levels off and goes around the ridge, through scrub oak. It passes a large outcropping of rock on the right. There are several nice camp spots along this section, as evidenced by the fire rings. Past the level section, the trail climbs gradually along the steep side of the hill. A fall would lead to a long tumble. There are a few open areas, but for the most part, from here to the end of the trail you will be hiking in shade. You are now very close to the radio towers. One appears to be about half a mile above you as you cross an open area across a slab of rocks. Past this slab of rocks, the trail climbs steeply for two hundred yards and reenters a thickly forested area, mostly fir and some oak. The trail in this section climbs gradually. It is smooth and covered with fir needles. It is so thick that the sunlight barely filters through. This is one of the prettiest sections of the trail. Basically the trail is a steep but gradual climb, with a few areas of very steep climbing. As the trail approaches the saddle, there are some huge fir trees near the top. As you come to the saddle, there are a number of signs. One trail leads to Knaage Trail and another to Peck Basin Overlook. Another sign indicates that Kellogg Mountain is .2 miles away. The metal Forest Service sign shows the way to Bigelow I.O. .4 miles. Soldier Camp is 5.2 miles back the way you just came. The Palisades Ranger Station is .5 miles down the hill. The last half-mile is through ponderosa pine, in an open, parklike area covered with ferns. You catch glimpses of Tucson and again get that island-in-the-sky feeling.

Civilization returns as you approach the Palisades Ranger Station, where you have to get in one car and retrieve the other.

The Santa Rita Mountains

For nearly three hundred years, men have sought the gold and silver in the Santa Rita Mountains. The Spanish were the first to look for the treasures.

A large silver strike in 1736, seventy miles south of Tucson, drew a number of Spanish settlers to the area. Many of them came from the Basque region of Spain, and in their explanation of the location of the strike they referred to it using a Basque term, *aritz onac,* or "place of the oaks." An etymologist from the Center for Basque Studies at the University of Nebraska, William A. Douglass, argues that this is the origin of the name Arizona.

The Spanish established a mission at Tumacacori and a presidio at Tubac, both in the shadow of the Santa Ritas. Jesuit priests sent Indian laborers to the mines in the Santa Rita Mountains in the 1700s. By the mid-1800s, Apache attacks had forced the abandonment of the mission and the presidio, as well as the attempts to mine.

When the area became part of the United States with the Gadsden Purchase, attempts were again made at ranching and mining. So rich were the Santa Cruz Valley and the Santa Rita Mountains that they were the scene of constant battles over ownership. Huge Spanish land grants were supposedly to be honored by the Mexican government and, later, by the United States government. Complicating matters were the heirs of the Baca Float, who claimed the land as replacement for land they had once claimed in New Mexico. The disputes went all the way to the United States Supreme Court and are too complicated to discuss here.

Eventually the heirs of the Baca Float got much of the land in the Santa Cruz Valley, but not without vigorous attempts to claim a large area of the Santa Ritas. In pursuing their claims, two men were sent to survey the mountains. Both were killed by Apaches. Mount Wrightson and Mount Hopkins bear their names. Suffice it to say that the riches of the Santa Rita Mountains brought out the worst in many men.

As most of the Apaches were confined to reservations, mining in the Santa Ritas boomed. Towns grew overnight. By 1879 Greaterville had a population of five hundred, a public school, a post office, and several saloons. Driving through what remains of the town, en route to a hiking trail, it is hard to visualize that it ever existed. On the north side of the Santa Ritas, the town of Helvetia boasted a population of four hundred by 1891. Today all that remains are a few buildings and a cemetery.

Look at the map of the Santa Ritas. Josephine Canyon, Gardner Canyon, and Temporal Gulch are dotted with mines. The Agua Caliente Trail passes the old Treasure Vault Mine. Florida Saddle Trail passes the workings of the old Florida Mine.

It did not last. By the early 1900s, most of the mines had played out. Helvetia and Greaterville are ghost towns. The hopes of many lie crushed in the tailings of the old mines. The Santa Ritas were made part of the Coronado National Forest in 1908 and are now a National Wilderness Area. The mines are closed forever.

The gold of the Santa Ritas now lies in the hiking trails and beautiful backcountry of the mountains. Although farthest from Tucson, the Santa Ritas provide excellent hiking. The trails that are reached from Interstate 19 and out of Madera Canyon are most easily accessible. The trails that come in from Patagonia and Sonoita require four-wheel drive and long drives to the trailheads. Many of the trails lead to Mount Wrightson, and several loop combinations can be worked out. The Santa Ritas are fun mountains to hike!

Old Baldy Trail

General Description
> A much-used trail to the summit of the highest peak in the Santa Rita Mountains, with spectacular views

Difficulty
> Difficult, some areas of exceptionally steep climbing

Best time of year to hike
> Spring, fall, summer

Length
> 5 miles

Elevation
> 5420 feet at trailhead; 9453 feet on summit

Miles to trailhead from Speedway/Campbell intersection
> 43.5

Directions to trailhead from Speedway/Campbell intersection
> Go west on Speedway until the intersection with I-10. Go east on I-10. Follow I-10 until the intersection with I-19 (the Nogales exit). Get on I-19 to Green Valley. From Green Valley, follow the brown signs to Madera Canyon, exiting at exit number 63. Turn left under I-19. Continue to follow the signs to Madera Canyon, through Continental, to the upper parking lot where the road comes to a dead end. A trails sign indicates parking. The Old Baldy trailhead is .3 miles on an old road at the south end of this parking lot.

One never knows exactly what to expect while hiking this popular Mount Wrightson trail. As I pulled in the parking lot at 7:00 A.M. one Sunday in early June, I was surprised to have difficulty finding a place to park. Then I discovered that a canopy had been set up and a wedding was in progress. About a mile into the hike I was nearly scared witless by a moving brown object that I thought was a bear. No, it was a man and his tripod, both completely covered with camouflage netting. Farther along the trail I met a backpacker with a full-sized guitar attached to his pack. At Bellows Spring a man was celebrating his sixtieth birthday by taking his poodle, complete with neckerchief, to "sign in" on the summit of Wrightson.

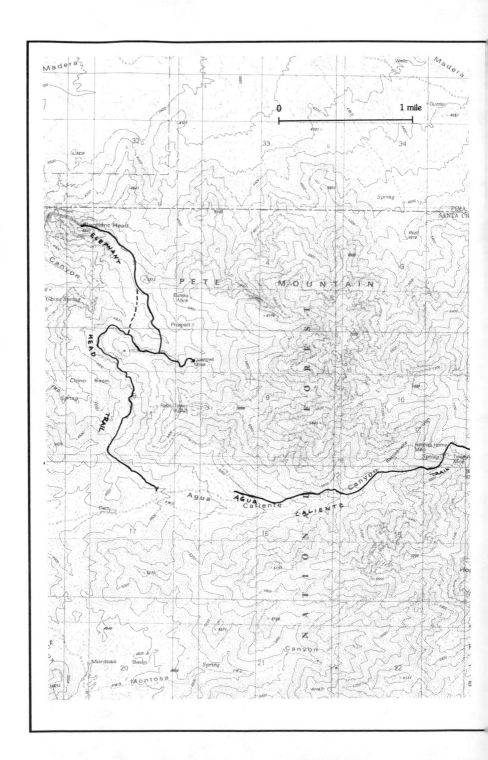

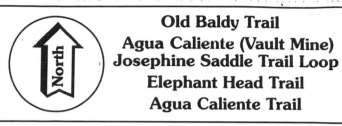

Old Baldy Trail
Agua Caliente (Vault Mine)
Josephine Saddle Trail Loop
Elephant Head Trail
Agua Caliente Trail

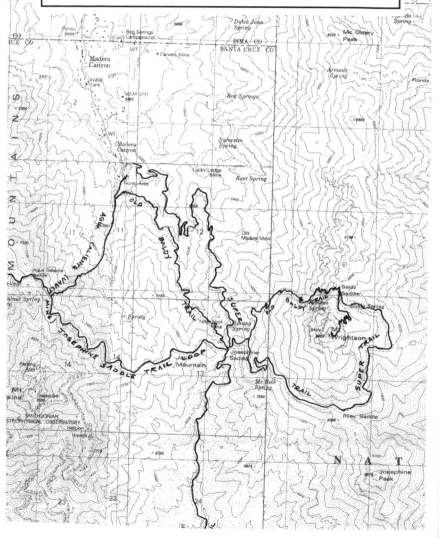

Mount Wrightson, Old Baldy Trail

(He made it, and I photographed him at the top!) Near Baldy
Saddle I had to dodge a group of runners returning from the
summit. One had made it to the top in one hour and thirty-six
minutes. It would take me nearly five hours!

The Old Baldy Trail to the summit of Mount Wrightson is the most
direct route to the 9,453-foot peak, the highest in the Santa Rita Mountain range. It is also the steepest and most difficult route. The trail name
refers to Old Baldy, the original name of Mount Wrightson. It was
renamed in memory of William Wrightson, who was killed by Apaches in
1865 as he was attempting to survey this area to establish the claims
of the Baca Float heirs. (His assistant, Gilbert Hopkins, was also
killed, and nearby Mount Hopkins was named in his honor.)

The trailhead is .3 miles up an old road that leaves from the
south end of the parking area. The Old Baldy Trail makes a sharp
left at a signed intersection. The signs in the Santa Rita Mountains
are superior to many signed trails. Made of metal, with the trail
name etched through the metal and attached by pipes set in
concrete, they are usually safe from man and beast!

The trail begins to climb immediately under a canopy of oak
trees. After about two hundred yards there is a large green water
tank to the left. This is the holding tank for the water that supplies
the homes and businesses in Madera Canyon.

This is a heavily used trail, and over the years many persons
have shortcut the trail. This unnecessary practice has caused
erosion, and in several areas the trail has been rerouted. The old
portion of the trail is often covered with dead limbs or otherwise
blocked so that the correct route is always easy to follow.

The trail continues to gain elevation quickly. One of the best
things about the Old Baldy Trail is the views. You can see Green
Valley, the pecan orchards, and the copper mines to the northwest.
As you get higher, you can see the telescopes atop Mount Hopkins
to the southwest.

Most of the trail follows the north or east side of the ridge.
There are several small drainages crossing the trail that may hold
water, depending on the time of year you are hiking. After about
one mile, you cross a large side drainage and then wind around the
east side of the hill to an open area once used as a helicopter landing pad. Past the open area, the trail reenters the forest, now con-
sisting of oak and ponderosa pine.

After crossing two small drainages, the trail goes slightly downhill, across a large drainage, and climbs along the side of the mountain. In this section the trail splits, and there is a rather distinct trail that goes to the left. The correct route is the wide trail straight ahead. There are several faint trails in this area that lead down to one of several secluded camp spots in the ravine. The correct trail continues along the west side of this ravine in a lovely area.

Soon the trail begins to switchback steeply. This is one area that has been rerouted, but the main trail is always evident. The switchbacks become longer and end at Josephine Saddle. It will take the average hiker two hours to reach the saddle.

Josephine Saddle is a crossroads for several trails. Josephine, the youngest daughter of the pioneer Pennington family, is well remembered in the Santa Ritas. She has a saddle, a canyon, and a peak named in her honor. The saddle is a beautiful area, covered with tall ponderosa pines. It is a favorite camping area, and it is a rare hike that you do not see a tent set up under a tree.

There are a number of signs in the saddle. The Old Baldy Trail leaves the saddle to the east, past the cross marking the death of three Boy Scouts who were camped in the vicinity of the saddle on 15 November 1958, when an unusually severe winter storm hit Tucson. The cross and plaque were placed there by their Boy Scout troop. Wreaths and flowers are frequently placed on the cross, which serves not only as a memorial but as a reminder of the dangers to those of us who hike and camp on this mountain.

A few yards past the memorial, the Temporal Canyon trail cuts off to the right. Follow the arrows to the left to Mount Wrightson. The trail to Baldy Saddle switchbacks gradually and is in this section sandy and smooth. After the second switchback, you can see the other side of the mountain, including the observatory on Mount Hopkins. The trail goes around the south side of the mountain and climbs gradually. After .8 miles you come to a sign indicating the cut-off of the Super Trail to the right. You want to continue left on the Old Baldy Trail. From here, Bellows Spring is 1.1 miles, Baldy Saddle 1.8, and the summit, 2.7. The trail continues to gain elevation, and the views are excellent as it works its way up the mountain. The vegetation is oak interspersed with ponderosa pine. It is a lovely area. The climb increases in steepness and shortly comes to a flat area with several large logs. This is a good campsite, with a large fire ring to the left of the trail.

Here the trail turns to the right sharply and switchbacks up the mountain. As the switchbacks get steeper, the views get better! There is a short level area for about a quarter of a mile, with Mount Wrightson towering above you, before the switchbacks begin again in earnest. Finally the trail levels out in the vicinity of Bellows Spring. Water is always flowing out of the pipe into a tank. Tempting as it is to drink the water, all wilderness water should be purified.

Past the spring the trail is very rocky and exceptionally pretty. It is a brushy trail with a series of short, rocky switchbacks. A few hundred yards past the spring is a stand of young aspen, but for the most part, the vegetation consists of thick shrubs. The views up this final section of the trail to Baldy Saddle are excellent. You are at about eye level with Mount Hopkins, site of the Smithsonian Institution and the University of Arizona Fred A. Whipple Observatory. To the northwest you can see another famous observatory, Kitt Peak. Baboquivari Peak, the sacred mountain of the Tohono O'odham tribe, is the bald, rounded summit southwest of Kitt Peak. From one vantage point, you can spot your car in the Madera Canyon parking lot.

As the switchbacks approach the saddle, you can see that there has been much shortcutting in the past. Excellent trail reconstruction has been done to discourage the practice and to make the final few switchbacks very evident. The saddle itself is beautiful, and the views to the east are impressive. The area is much used as a camping spot. Even on the hottest summer day in Tucson, the temperature in the 8,050-foot saddle is delightful.

From the saddle it is .9 miles to the summit of Mount Wrightson. The trail begins at the south end of the saddle, and for nearly half a mile it is gradual, along the side of the mountain. It goes through tall ponderosa pine, and the trail is covered with pine needles, making it a welcome change. Of course, this cannot last, and the trail quickly becomes a series of rocky switchbacks with only one break to the top. A wooden sign is at the half-mile point. From the sign, which because it is one of the few wooden signs in the Santa Ritas, may not be there when you attempt the hike, it is half a mile to the top. This rocky, steep trail rounds to the south side of the mountain and climbs to the summit.

The summit of Mount Wrightson has views that on a clear day are spectacular. Take a map with you and spend some time picking out the various mountain ranges and the sights that you can see from the top. The foundations of an old Forest Service lookout are on the summit, as is a boxed trail sign.

Only two things can mar the feeling of accomplishment that you have in climbing this summit. First, if you should be there in June, the ladybugs claim this summit as their own, as do millions of small insects. Having been warned by hikers coming down from the top, I covered myself with insect repellent, and the bugs loved it! A second problem is the air pollution that too frequently obscures the view.

But on a clear day, standing atop Mount Wrightson, you can understand why people get married in its shadow and carry guitars and poodles to the top. It is still hard, however, to understand why anyone runs to the summit!

Agua Caliente (Vault Mine) Josephine Saddle Trail Loop

General Description
A little-used trail past an old mine that provides outstanding views

Difficulty
Difficult, some areas of exceptionally steep climbing

Best time of year to hike
Spring, fall, summer

Length
6.1 miles Old Baldy return; 7.4 miles Super Trail return

Elevation
5420 feet at trailhead; 7300 feet at highest intersection

Miles to trailhead from Speedway/Campbell intersection
43.5

Directions to trailhead from Speedway/Campbell intersection
Go west on Speedway until the intersection with I-10. Go east on I-10. Follow I-10 until the intersection with I-19 (the Nogales exit). Remain on I-19 until you reach Green Valley. Follow the brown signs to Madera Canyon, exiting at exit number 63. Turn left under I-19. Continue to follow the signs to Madera Canyon, through Continental, to the upper parking lot where the road comes to a dead end. A sign indicates parking for trails. The Agua Caliente (Vault Mine) Trail leaves from the south end of the parking lot.

"Tips for Hikers," published by the Friends of Madera Canyon and available at the parking area, does not recommend hiking the Agua Caliente (Vault Mine) Trail. The directional sign placed at the intersection warns that the trail is "VERY STEEP." True, the trail does climb fourteen hundred feet in .6 miles and it is VERY STEEP; but, as a loop trail through Josephine Saddle, it is one of the prettiest hikes leading out of Madera Canyon.

The Agua Caliente Trail begins .6 miles up the old road that leads south from the parking area. At .3 miles you come to the first

Hiker looking in Treasure Vault mine—Agua Caliente (Vault Mine) Trail

trail intersection. To the left is the Old Baldy Trail to Josephine
Saddle. Continue up the road following the sign to Agua Caliente
Trail, the one indicated on the sign as being a Very Steep Trail. The
old road parallels Madera Creek. Usually there is some water
flowing in the stream. Tall Arizona sycamores and several varieties
of oak shade the area. Over two hundred species of birds have
been spotted in Madera Canyon, including the rare and colorful
elegant trogon.

As the road steepens, keep looking for a side trail on the right
that crosses the stream. This area is used heavily, and there are
many side trails leading down to the stream. The correct trail crosses
Madera Creek and passes to the right of a large oak tree. In about
two hundred yards a sign indicates that the Agua Caliente Trail is to
the right. From here it is 3.2 miles to Josephine Saddle.

Past the sign the trail soon follows a ledge far above Madera
Creek. This is a beautiful area, with large oaks and ponderosa pine.
It is level only a short distance before beginning a series of steep
switchbacks. After the first set of switchbacks, the trail comes to an
open area, and you can see the Catalina Mountains and part of
Tucson before the trail again switchbacks up the hill. Unfortunately,

there has been a lot of shortcutting on the trail. It is hard to understand why anyone would want to shortcut when the trail is already very steep.

As the trail rounds to the east side of the mountain, it opens up and the trees are not as thick. It is again very rocky and steep. After .6 miles and a fourteen hundred-foot elevation gain, you come to an abandoned mine tunnel.

This is part of the workings of the Treasure Vault Mine, discovered in 1899 and owned by the Santa Rita Mining Company. Mining in this area dates to the arrival of the Jesuit fathers in the early 1700s, who used Indian labor to search for gold and silver. However, by the time of the Gadsden Purchase in 1853, when this area became part of the United States, Apache raids made mining too dangerous. It was not until after the Civil War that American miners once again entered the area. A little farther up the trail and down to the left is the lower tunnel, originally 135 feet long. No production data is available, so it is not known if the miners who originally hiked this "very steep trail" made a profit for the Santa Rita Mining Company.

The trail beyond the mine, with the exception of the first two hundred yards, is exceptionally steep and rocky. At 1.2 miles you come to a signed intersection. Turn left to Josephine Saddle.

Now the steep part of the trail is over as it circles the mostly open, northeast side of the mountain. Although there are a few steep dropoffs and several areas where the trail crosses rockfall, the trail is a joy to hike from here to Josephine Saddle.

During the first part of this section of the trail, there are some very large oak trees. There are hundreds of tiny oak trees along the trail, so thick that in several places you put your foot down with the hope that there is not a rattler shading himself! The trail goes in and out of cover, under huge box elder and a few ponderosa. In spring the pink blossoms of locust trees lend a pleasant fragrance to the air. There is a section of large, beautiful aspen, one of the few areas of aspen in the Santa Ritas.

After you have hiked for about one and one-half miles, there is a trail to the right that eventually goes up to Mount Hopkins. It is interesting to go the hundred yards or so to the top of the ridge. The road up Mount Hopkins is clearly visible, as are several buildings and what looks like the back of one of the observatory telescopes. There are several huge alligator juniper trees, including one at least six feet in diameter.

Past this lookout point, the trail goes downhill gradually and comes to a short saddle before once again gaining in elevation. There is an open area covered with ferns that looks like it was once a burn area. Past this burn area, the trail reenters the woods and goes downhill gradually until it reaches Josephine Saddle.

As you will see, Josephine Saddle is a crossroads for many trails and makes it possible to hike with any number of loops. For this particular loop, you may return to the parking area via the Old Baldy Trail or the Super Trail. The choice depends on the condition of your legs and the amount of time you have allotted for hiking.

Elephant Head Trail

General Description
A bushwack, partly on old mine roads, to the top of an unusual rock formation that, from some viewpoints, resembles the head of a giant elephant

Difficulty
Moderate, some areas of steep climbing

Best time of year to hike
Spring, fall, winter

Length
4 miles

Elevation
4580 feet at trailhead; 5641 feet at high point

Miles to trailhead from Speedway/Campbell intersection
44

Directions to trailhead from Speedway/Campbell intersection
Go west on Speedway to Interstate 10. Follow I-10 east (El Paso) to the Nogales exit, I-19. Go south on I-19 past Green Valley to the Canoa exit, number 56. Turn left under the highway, following signs to Elephant Head Road. At the intersection, turn right to Elephant Head Road, a distance of 3 miles. Turn left on Elephant Head Road. After you cross the Santa Cruz River and the railroad tracks, watch carefully on the right for Mt. Hopkins Road. Turn right on Mt. Hopkins Road for 5.5 miles to Forest Service Road 183. The sign will say Agua Caliente Canyon and KMSB and will turn to the left. Take Forest Service Road 183 for 2½ miles. Right before the road makes a sharp left and begins the climb to the television towers, there is a large parking area on the right. Park here for the route to Elephant Head. A high-clearance vehicle is required for Forest Service Road 183.

At the base of the Santa Rita Mountains, to the northwest, between Mount Hopkins and Interstate 19, is what appears to be a mountain of rock. From some viewpoints the formation resembles

Elephant Head is formation on the left—Elephant Head Trail

the head of a giant elephant and, although early maps of the area refer to it as Old Pete Mountain, the formation today is called Elephant Head. It appears impossible to climb, but it is actually relatively accessible from the eastern approach.

From the parking area, cross the road and look on the right for a trail constructed by the Greater Arizona Bicycling Association. It is marked with a flexible brown sign. This leads directly to the saddle at the top of the ridge.

At the saddle a path descends to another old mine road. Turn right on this road. The basin below was at one time a very active copper, silver, gold, and lead mining area. Worked by Chinese laborers, the basin became known as Chino, Spanish for "Chinese." China Spring and Chino Canyon also derive their names from the Chinese workers. As the trail flattens out, the bike trail turns left, again marked by a flexible sign. Watch this spot on your return as it is easy to miss this turnoff and end up in Chino Basin. Your route is to continue straight ahead and climb the other side of the basin on what was once a road to the Quantrell Mine. As you walk the mine road, look carefully along the side of the road, and you will see some remaining evidence of the hand-stacked rock berm built by the Chinese workers. There are still a few active claims in this basin.

As the road ascends the ridge, it winds to the southeast, eventually ending at the site of the old Quantrell Mine. As the road reaches the peak of the ridge, the views are magnificent. You can see Kitt Peak, Baboquivari, the copper mines near Green Valley, the small town of Amado, and, finally, Elephant Head. Look north to Elephant Head and the ridge to its right. Exactly how you get to the saddle southeast of Elephant Head depends on how far down you go before beginning to climb again. The shortest route requires the most elevation loss and gain. The longest but easiest route continues along the jeep road that approaches the mine before crossing the canyon.

Once across the canyon, my advice is to stay low enough to keep Elephant Head in view, so as not to lose your perspective and go too high. I like to "bite the bullet" and drop steeply into the canyon about a mile before reaching the mine. This quick drop results in an equally quick, steep climb to the ridge right below Elephant Head. Although this climb must be made very carefully, it appears more difficult than it is, and the resulting views from the summit are worth every step.

This hike is decidedly different from the other hikes in this guide. There is no definite trail, the summit is a bald outcropping of rock, and much of the area is scarred by mining, yet it is part of the terrain of the Santa Rita Mountains that should not be missed.

Agua Caliente Trail

General Description
> A scenic, little-used trail to a beautiful saddle

Difficulty
> Moderate, some areas of steep climbing

Best time of year to hike
> Spring, fall

Length
> 1.7 miles

Elevation
> 4580 feet at trailhead; 7260 feet at Agua Caliente Saddle

Miles to trailhead from Speedway/Campbell intersection
> 44

Directions to trailhead from Speedway/Campbell intersection
> Go west on Speedway to Interstate 10. Follow I-10 east
> (to El Paso) to the Nogales exit, I-19. Go south on I-19
> past Green Valley to the Canoa exit, number 56. Turn left
> under the highway, following signs to Elephant Head Road.
> At the intersection, turn right to Elephant Head Road, a
> distance of 3 miles. Turn left on Elephant Head Road. After
> you cross the Santa Cruz River and the railroad tracks,
> watch carefully on the right for Mt. Hopkins Road. Turn
> right on Mt. Hopkins Road for 5.5 miles to Forest Service
> Road 183. The sign will say Agua Caliente Canyon and
> KMSB and will turn to the left. Take Forest Service Road
> 183 for 2½ miles. The trailhead is on the right, about half
> a mile after the road crosses Agua Caliente Canyon and
> begins the steep climb to the television towers. A large
> metal sign by the side of the road marks the beginning of
> the Agua Caliente Saddle Trail. There is not a parking area,
> but there is room to pull your vehicle to the side of the
> road. A high clearance vehicle is required for Forest Service
> Road 183.

Agua Caliente—"hot water" in Spanish—is the name given to
the canyon between Mount Hopkins and Elephant Head. The spring

View from beginning of Agua Caliente Trail

that gives the canyon its name is at the mouth of the canyon and, according to a geothermal survey by the Arizona Geological Survey, is more warm than hot, never rising above one hundred degrees. Although it is a long drive to the trailhead to hike a relatively short trail, the hike to Agua Caliente Saddle provides a different perspective on the Santa Ritas and gives the hiker a better understanding of the size of the range.

The trail goes along the north side of Agua Caliente Canyon and is at times rocky. Most of the year there will be some water running in the canyon. There are excellent views of the Smithsonian Institution's Fred A. Whipple Observatory on top of Mount Hopkins. Observe it carefully and you will see that the entire building changes position, and at times there appears to be an opening in the building.

As the trail winds its way out of the canyon, the vegetation changes from scrub oak to ponderosa pine, and the rocky trail gives way to a smooth, pine-covered surface. There is some evidence of the mining that was the original purpose of this trail. A series of steep switchbacks brings you to Agua Caliente Saddle.

The saddle is a lovely area that is infrequently used. There is an exceptionally large alligator juniper just before you reach the saddle. There are several good areas for camping.

From the saddle it is .8 miles of gradual uphill to the intersection with the Vault Mine Trail. From this intersection the Agua Caliente Trail continues 2.2 miles to Josephine Saddle. This portion of the Agua Caliente Trail is described in the Vault Mine Trail description. By careful study of a trail map of the Santa Ritas, you can work out any number of hiking combinations.

Super Trail

General Description
A practically painless way to climb to the summit of Mount Wrightson, this is a gradual trail with some especially beautiful sections

Difficulty
Moderate, very gradual ascent

Best time of year to hike
Spring, fall, summer

Length
8.2 miles

Elevation
5240 feet at trailhead; 9453 feet on summit

Miles to trailhead from Speedway/Campbell intersection
43.5

Directions to trailhead from Speedway/Campbell intersection
Go west on Speedway until the intersection with I-10. Turn east on I-10. Follow I-10 until the intersection with I-19 (the Nogales exit). Follow I-19 to Green Valley. From Green Valley, follow the brown signs to Madera Canyon, exiting at exit number 63. Turn left under I-19. Continue following the signs to Madera Canyon, through Continental, to the upper parking lot where the road comes to a dead end. A Trails sign indicates parking. The Super Trail trailhead is at the northeast corner of the parking lot.

The Super Trail begins to the left of the parking area and is marked by a trail information board and a metal sign. This exceptionally pretty trail is the easiest, but longest, route to the summit of Mount Wrightson.

The trail parallels the right side of the creek, which has water much of the year. There are nice camping spots beside the creek. The trail passes under tall oaks, juniper pines, and Arizona sycamores. After a quarter of a mile, the trail crosses the creek and heads to the left, in the first of several long, gradual switchbacks. As you turn on the second switchback, there are excellent views of the final goal—Mount Wrightson.

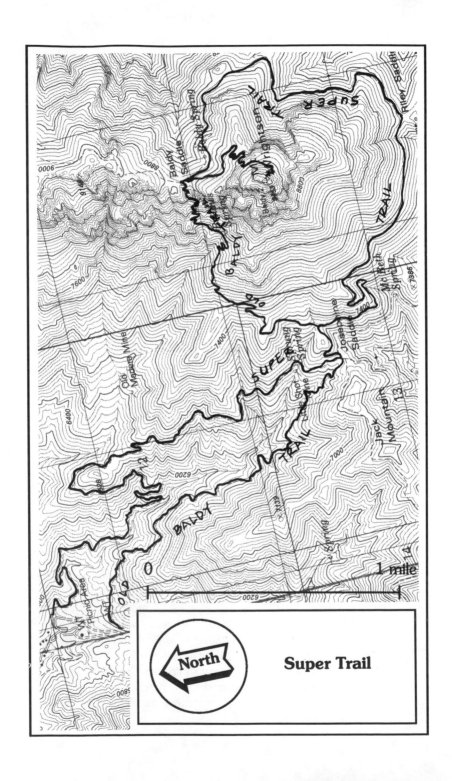

Super Trail

Unfortunately this first section has been shortcut often, and there is quite a bit of erosion. The elevation gain is so gradual that almost without realizing it, you are high above the canyon.

The trail goes in and out of shady areas with several varieties of oak and a few ponderosa pine. Several side ravines cross the trail. At certain times of year there is water trickling down these ravines. Whatever time of year, the drainages make very green, pretty areas, often with wildflowers growing. Mount Wrightson pops in and out of view as the trail once again begins to parallel the creek. The creek by now will have small pools in all but the driest of seasons.

After about half a mile, the trail again leaves the creek and begins to switchback up the side of the canyon. As you gain in elevation, the views of the valley and the canyon are wider. Green Valley, the dark green of the pecan orchards, and the mines are clearly visible. One long switchback heads north, away from Josephine Saddle, and comes to a point of the ridge. Here the views of the valley are especially impressive.

As the trail rounds the ridge and once again heads south toward Josephine Saddle, it reenters a shady area with pines and a few spruce trees. The trail opens up briefly, and now you can see the observatory on top of Mount Hopkins. Also you can look down on the Old Baldy Trail headed to Josephine Saddle on the other side of the canyon.

At the three-mile point a wooden sign was at one time placed in the fork of a tree. The tree has grown and imbedded the sign firmly in its trunk. From the sign it is only one mile to Josephine Saddle.

Past the sign is another exceptionally pretty area. There are pines, oaks, and an occasional open area. Two-tenths of a mile before Josephine Saddle is Sprung Spring. A round metal tank with water piped in is a welcome sight. It is always running, and although it should be purified before drinking, it is nice to know that this permanent source of water is available. The water is cold, even on a hot June day. The trees surrounding the spring are tall, and the vegetation is lush. This is a great area for wildlife spotting, especially in the early evening.

Past the spring the trail switchbacks quickly into Josephine Saddle, coming out right at the sign that marks the death of three Boy Scouts who were camped in the vicinity of the saddle on 15 November 1958, when an unusually severe winter storm hit Tucson.

*This memorial is on the Super Trail—it has been here over 30 years
and always has flowers.*

At this crossroads it is possible to leave the Super Trail and continue your ascent of Mount Wrightson by the Old Baldy Trail. This would shorten the hike considerably, but add greatly to the steepness. I'll assume that you plan to go all the way to Baldy Saddle via the Super Trail. To do this, turn left at the signed intersection, following the arrow to Mount Wrightson. The trail switchbacks to the left and then quickly to the right. Continue up this switchback for approximately two hundred yards to another signed intersection. Follow the sign to the right to continue your climb to Mount Wrightson via the Super Trail. From this point it is another 4.2 miles to the summit. The ascent is so gradual that this is practically a painless way to attain Baldy Saddle. Unfortunately, there is no painless way to make it to the summit of Mount Wrightson!

At first the trail climbs in a series of long, easy switchbacks and crosses a rocky area. From all along this portion of the trail there are excellent views of Mount Hopkins. The observatory atop Mount Hopkins is a joint venture of the University of Arizona and the Simthsonian Institution. Don't be surprised if you think the building is positioned differently at times—the entire building rotates when the telescopes are rotated. (The only known insurance claim filed for a building hitting a car involved this building.)

As the trail winds around the mountain, there are a couple of spots where the trail crosses rock falls. A tumble down the rocks could be a bad experience. For about a mile the trail goes through a grassy area with a few pine and scrub oak. The basic plan of the trail is to go around the south side of Mount Wrightson. A trail cuts off to the right across Riley Saddle to Josephine Peak. You should continue straight ahead. Past the trail intersection, the trail continues to gradually work its way around the mountain, arriving at the drainage that comes down from Mount Wrightson. Here are large rocks, a large alligator juniper, and a huge ponderosa pine. Farther up the drainage, you can see a stand of aspen.

The trail leaves this drainage and continues through an open area to a trail intersection. The trail to the right leads off to Gardner Canyon. You should continue left and around Mount Wrightson.

Soon you leave the open and come into a exceptionally pretty area. Several long switchbacks lead through tall ponderosas and beautiful Douglas fir trees to Baldy Saddle. Just before reaching Baldy Spring there is an oft-used campsite with logs for sitting and the ever-present fire ring. Almost immediately past this campsite is

Baldy Spring. The tank is nearly always full, and the water can be used if it is purified. A half-mile from the spring and you are at Baldy Saddle. The Super Trail ends at Baldy Saddle and you can turn left and join the Old Baldy Trail to the summit.

The return from Mount Wrightson can be down the Super Trail, the Old Baldy Trail, or a combination of the two. If the entire hike is done on the Super Trail, it is a total of 16.4 miles. That makes for a very long hike, regardless of how gradual the climb. Most hikers prefer to work out the combination that most suits their hiking style. Most prefer to hike up to Josephine Saddle on the Old Baldy Trail, and from the saddle to Baldy Saddle on the Super Trail. The return trip can be down the first segment of the Old Baldy Trail to Josephine Saddle, and from Josephine Saddle to the parking area on the Super Trail, or whatever combination suits you best.

Florida Saddle Trail

General Description

A steep hike through a beautiful canyon, along open hillsides, to a thickly forested saddle

Difficulty

Difficult, some areas of exceptionally steep climbing

Best time of year to hike

Spring, fall

Length

5.2 miles to Florida Saddle

Elevation

4340 feet at the trailhead; 7820 feet at the saddle

Miles to trailhead from Speedway/Campbell intersection

42.6

Directions to trailhead from Speedway/Campbell intersection

Go west on Speedway until the intersection with I-10. Turn east on I-10. Follow I-10 until the intersection with I-19 (the Nogales exit). Get on I-19 to Green Valley. In Green Valley, follow the brown signs to Madera Canyon, exiting at exit number 63. Turn left under I-19, continuing to follow the signs to Madera Canyon. Seven miles past Continental, the Box Canyon Road (Forest Service Road 62) turns left. This road is unpaved, but it is suitable for passenger cars. Drive 3.1 miles. The trailhead parking area is on the left, immediately before the entrance to the Florida Work Center.

This trail is not Florida as in the state, but *Florida,* as in Spanish for "flower." Miners working here in the 1880s probably named the canyon for the abundant flowers. Rarely will you meet a fellow hiker on this trail, as most hikers approach the Santa Ritas from Madera Canyon.

A man named Charles Robinson owned nine claims in this area in the 1880s. By the early 1900s, the Florida Mine had three fifty- to one hundred-foot tunnels and shallow shafts. The miners lived in Robinson Camp near a spring and received their mail from the nearby boomtown of Helvetia. Production at the mine did not meet expectations, and only 140 tons of copper ore were ever produced.

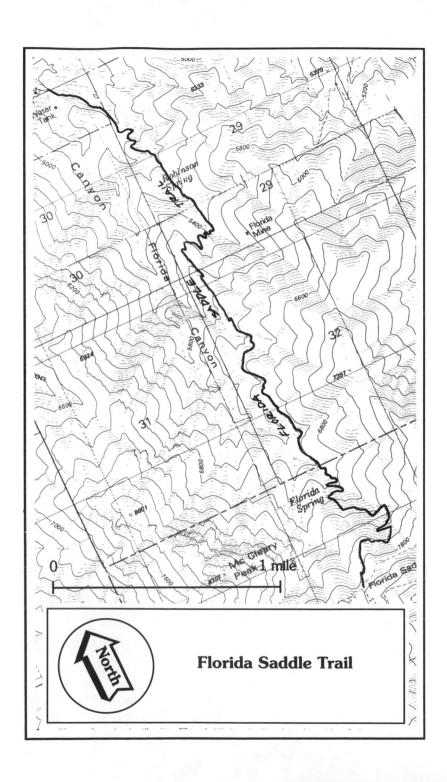

Florida Saddle Trail

From the parking area, the trail immediately crosses the creek and starts up a road. It parallels a fence on a narrow rocky trail, past two rectangular concrete stock tanks. As the trail climbs a brief rise, the buildings of the Santa Rita Experimental Range facility can be seen on your right. The Experimental Range is administered by the University of Arizona College of Agriculture. This is an unusual area in that the tall trees growing in the canyon on the right contrast sharply with the huge prickly pear and ocotillo on the left.

In .3 miles you reach a hinged gate, which is the entry to the Coronado National Forest. Across the creek bed is a sign indicating the beginning of the Florida Saddle Trail. From this point it is 4.2 miles to Florida Saddle. The trail crosses the stream several times, but most of the year the stream will be dry. There are several rock dams wired together with fencing material that occasionally back up pools of water. An empty round stock tank is on the right of the trail. The vegetation is mostly scrub oak intertwined with grapevines.

After not quite a mile, the trail leaves the creek bed and begins to climb out of the bottom of the canyon. As you climb, you begin to get good views of the valley to the north. At the top of another rise is a round stock tank, this one very much in use. Cattle roam this area, as evidenced by the droppings around the tank. From here, there are more good views of the valley.

The switchbacks level out and the trail continues uphill. The vegetation changes to include pinon pine and alligator juniper. The trail drops down slightly into an area known as Robinson Spring, named after Charles Robinson. At even the driest time of year there will be some moisture in the area and many colorful flowers.

Past the spring the trail enters a lovely area, with tall Arizona sycamores and a canopy of oak trees. It continues to climb under the trees for about one-quarter of a mile. Past this area the trail switchbacks up to the top of what appears to be a tailings pile from the old mines. For a brief period the trail levels off and enters some fir trees. Past this fir tree section, it opens up again and switchbacks steeply up the side of the hill. The trail is rocky and at times hard to climb. It tops a ridge to an area that has been cleared. Here a trail leads off to the right to a campsite. The correct route is uphill, to the left. The views from this cleared area are excellent, both into the valley and into Florida Canyon to the west.

A cool camping spot—Florida Saddle Trail

After another quarter of a mile of climbing through manzanita and scrub oak, the trail reenters a shady area with some ponderosa pine and fir. A partially buried water pipe follows the trail, which soon drops down into a grassy ravine. This is near Florida Spring. Most of the year there will be some water trickling. Again, flowers grow in abundance. Across the drainage and around the basin, the trail enters a section with huge fir trees.

From here to the saddle the trail is exceptionally pretty as it goes under the huge fir trees and a few ponderosa pines. The switchbacks are long and steep and, although pleasant to hike, it is not an easy portion of the trail. You pass an area used by campers, with some big logs and boards for seats. The trail climbs this north side of the mountain in a series of long switchbacks. A final long switchback to the right brings you to the saddle. A beautiful spot used for camping, this saddle is the intersection for several trails and is often used as a connecting loop with the Josephine Saddle trails.

Josephine Canyon Trail

General Description

One of the most beautiful canyons in the Santa Ritas

Difficulty

Moderate, some areas of steep climbing

Best time of year to hike

Spring, fall

Length

2.8 miles from trailhead to Josephine Saddle—add additional miles depending on how far you walk on the jeep road

Elevation

5720 feet at trailhead; 7100 feet at Josephine Saddle

Miles to trailhead from Speedway/Campbell intersection

71

Directions to trailhead from Speedway/Campbell intersection

Go west on Speedway until the intersection with I-10. Follow I-10 22 miles until Arizona State Route 83 exits south to Sonoita. It is 27 miles from I-10 to Sonoita. From Sonoita, follow Arizona State Route 82 for 13 miles southwest to Patagonia. From the junction of Fourth Avenue and State Route 82 in Patagonia, drive north two blocks and turn left on Pennsylvania Avenue. Cross Sonoita Creek and drive west past the Nature Conservancy area. This is Forest Service Road 143. Continue on FS 143, going left at the Squaw Gulch Road intersection. About 5 miles past this intersection there is a "Y" fork. Take the right fork. In not quite a mile you will come to Alto Camp, marked by a large Forest Service sign and a crumbling old adobe structure. In two more miles FS 143 turns left to I-19 and is now called the Bull Springs Road. (The Bull Springs Road requires rugged four-wheel drive but can be used as the route to the Josephine Canyon trailhead.) To reach the trailhead, bear right and continue for two miles on what is now FS 133. You may prefer to walk this last two miles; however, with a good four-wheel drive the road is easily passable. The trailhead is on the right, about half a mile

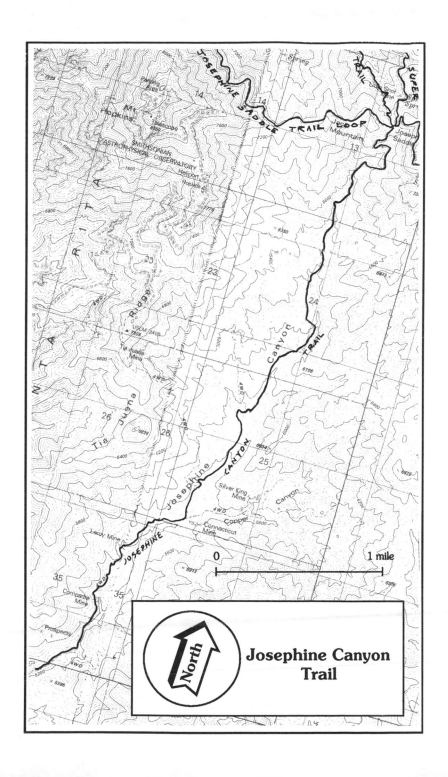

Josephine Canyon Trail

*past a large mine on the east side of the canyon, right
before the jeep road turns left and begins uphill. It is
marked by a metal forest service sign. The condition of the
road deteriorates rapidly by the time you reach the trailhead. (Note: The Forest Service has maps of all Forest
Service roads.)*

Josephine Canyon is in the heart of the previously rich mining
region of the Santa Rita Mountains. Steeped in legend and fact, the
canyon is extraordinarily scenic. It is so difficult to get to that it is
tempting to ignore this trail, but once done, you'll figure out a way
to do it again.

Plan on an entire day for this hike. The drive to the trailhead
takes over two hours. The road is moderately hilly, much of the
time fine for a passenger car, but I strongly recommend a truck or
four-wheel drive. The road goes through dramatically beautiful ranch
country. Tall waving grass and ranches tucked on the sides of hills
or in canyons could be part of a documentary on the West.
Although this is a long drive to reach a trailhead, the drive itself is
an adventure and well worth the time spent.

As you leave Patagonia, you pass the Nature Conservancy's
Patagonia-Sonoita Creek Sanctuary. The sanctuary protects 312
acres of riparian woodland between Patagonia and the Santa Rita
Mountains. Huge trees—cottonwood, white oak, walnut, alder, Arizona sycamore—provide a haven for over two hundred species of
birds as well as other wildlife.

Farther along Forest Service Road 143 there is much evidence
of the mining that first attracted non-Indians to this region. About
ten miles from Patagonia and on the right is the abandoned town of
Salero. Jesuit priests first directed mining in this location in the early
1700s. According to legend, the name is derived from a visit to the
mission at Tumacacori from the bishop of Sonora. During a feast in
his honor, the bishop noted the lack of a saltcellar, a small vessel,
traditionally made of silver, for holding salt. The humiliated padre in
charge dispatched a few men to the Santa Ritas to mine some silver
and fashion a saltcellar; thus the name *salero,* Spanish for "salt
pan." By 1857 a Cincinnati, Ohio, firm had acquired the mine
property. A post office was established in 1884 and remained in use
until 1890. Through many changes in ownership and relocations,

Remains of miner's cabin along Josephine Canyon Trail

the Salero site was active into the early part of this century. Although it is tempting to explore Salero, it is private property and is guarded by a caretaker.

A word of caution: all along the road are signs warning No Trespassing and No Hunting. Don't even think of not obeying them. This can be dangerous country, and, as a sign indicates as you enter the Salero Ranch farther on, lives have been lost in this area. The sign refers to the murder of two ranch hands during a robbery attempt in 1982.

Past the Salero Ranch is what remains of Alto Camp. The walls of a large adobe building are all that is left of the once thriving mining community. The structure had two functions. It was both the home of Josiah Bond, a mining engineer, schoolteacher, and some-time poet, and the local post office. Bond's wife, Minnie, doubled as a schoolteacher and postmistress. In 1922, Minnie was killed by lightning as she rode home from the day's classes. Bond lived in the home until his death in 1938. It was his dream that the road past his house would become the major thoroughfare connecting Nogales and Tucson.

Beyond Alto Camp the route, far from being a major thorough-fare, is nearly abandoned. Overgrown side roads lead to mines.

Names such as Eureka, Jefferson, Trenton, Bland, Wandering Jew, Compadre, and Royal Blue dot the map. What remains today varies. There may be a large tailings heap and little else, or the foundations of mine buildings. As you near the trailhead, a large mine, the Connecticut, is on the right. All of these mines have warning signs explaining the dangers of exploration. Do not risk becoming a statistic by ignoring the warnings.

The Forest Service sign indicating the trailhead is on the right, about half a mile past the Connecticut Mine and just before the road starts uphill. Although the road deteriorates considerably as it approaches the trailhead, it is possible to drive to this point if you have a sturdy vehicle. The sign indicates that it is 2.8 miles to Josephine Saddle. It is fun to work out a car shuttle and hike the entire five miles across to Madera Canyon.

As the trail enters the canyon, you immediately get an idea of how beautiful this hike will be. The smooth trail goes along the west side of the hill above the stream. In about half a mile you come to an area above a large waterfall, and if you have the time, it is fun to bushwack down to this area. The canyon is fairly wide at this point, and the vegetation is mostly scrub oak. There are large grassy areas, and this is an excellent feeding area for deer. It is a rare hike through this canyon that you would not see a deer or two.

The trail goes up and down gradually, crossing and recrossing the stream and side drainages. Occasionally Mount Wrightson and Josephine Peak come into view. In about a mile you come to the foundation of an old stone cabin. Across the stream is the remains of another small cabin. There are several large alligator junipers around the cabin sites. With the tall trees and the rushing water, we would think of this as a lovely retreat, but it is likely that the miners who once lived here viewed the area differently.

Past the cabin site, the trail begins to climb more sharply, occasionally switchbacking to climb higher, crossing the main stream and side streams. The trail is alternately smooth and rocky in this portion. There are large Arizona sycamores and some of the largest alligator junipers I have seen.

As you continue up the canyon, it becomes a paradise. Grapevines, tall ponderosa pines, several varieties of oak, clusters of Arizona bamboo, and cascading water create a mini-oasis. Birds abound and the wildflowers are spectacular. The beautiful canyon narrows, and finally the trail begins a sharp climb to Josephine

Saddle. The trail is now narrow and often covered with pine needles or oak leaves, making it easy to slip.

As the trail approaches the saddle, it becomes very narrow but is always easy to follow. Josephine Saddle is a major crossroads. From here you can continue the climb to the top of Mount Wrightson, go down to Madera Canyon, or around the Agua Caliente Trail. If you want to see Josephine Canyon without the long drive off paved roads, it is possible to hike to Josephine Canyon from Madera Canyon, as in the Old Baldy Trail or Super Trail hikes, and then hike down Josephine Canyon, returning to Madera Canyon.

Josephine, were she alive today, would certainly appreciate the beauty of the canyon named for her. It is generally believed that it was named for Josephine Pennington, daughter of the well-known pioneer family that settled and mined in the region in the mid-1800s.

Elias Green Pennington left his home state of South Carolina to settle in Texas. When civilization hemmed him in, he moved on. By 1857 he had started over the Gila Trail to California with his wife and eight children. When his wife died, Elias stopped at Fort Buchanan, Arizona. The Penningtons stayed and cut hay for the army, eventually moving twenty-five miles south of Fort Buchanan to a small house on the banks of the Santa Cruz River, eleven miles southeast of Calabazas. Here they built irrigation ditches and cultivated fields. Josephine was two years old at this time.

Never one to remain settled for long, Elias soon moved to a farm near the Sopori Ranch, ten miles northwest of Tubac. He operated a sawmill in Tucson, hauling lumber in from the Santa Ritas. The street on which the sawmill was located is now named Pennington.

Tragedy stalked the family. Daughter Anne died of malaria in 1867, and son James was killed by Apaches in 1868. When, in 1869, Elias and another son, Green, were killed by Apaches as they plowed the field, the remaining family moved to Tucson. Another daughter died later in an attempted move to California. Finally the four younger daughters, Josephine included, moved back to Texas to live with their brother, Jack, who had returned there in 1866.

Of all the Penningtons, why does Josephine's name live on in the Santa Ritas? Was she the beautiful sweetheart of a miner who longed for her? Perhaps as beautiful as the canyon that bears her name?

Kent Springs–Bog Springs Trail Loop

General Description
> A loop trail past three springs through an unusually lush area

Difficulty
> Moderate, some areas of steep climbing

Best time of year to hike
> Spring, fall, winter

Length
> 5.7 miles

Elevation
> 4820 feet at trailhead; 6620 feet at high point

Miles to trailhead from Speedway/Campbell intersection
> 42

Directions to trailhead from Speedway/Campbell intersection
> Go west on Speedway until the intersection with I-10.
> Follow I-10 east to the intersection with I-19 (the Nogales
> exit). Get on I-19 to Green Valley. From Green Valley,
> follow the brown signs to Madera Canyon, exiting at exit
> number 63. Go left under I-19, following the signs to
> Madera Canyon, through Continental, to a parking area to
> the right of the sign for Bog Springs Campground. This
> campground is on the left at the lower end of Madera
> Canyon, so look for it carefully as you enter the canyon. (If
> you choose to park in the campground, you must pay the
> $5 camping/ picnicking fee.) There is a parking area on the
> right, across from the campground entry sign.

The Kent Springs–Bog Springs Trail Loop is one of the prettiest
hikes in the Santa Rita Mountains. A series of springs create an
unusually lush area that attracts a large number of birds and wildlife.
Large Arizona sycamore and walnut trees provide a canopy that
invite you to relax and spend the better part of a day before returning to the arid environment of southeastern Arizona.

If you choose to park outside of the campground, locate the
trail by crossing the road at the upper end of the parking area and

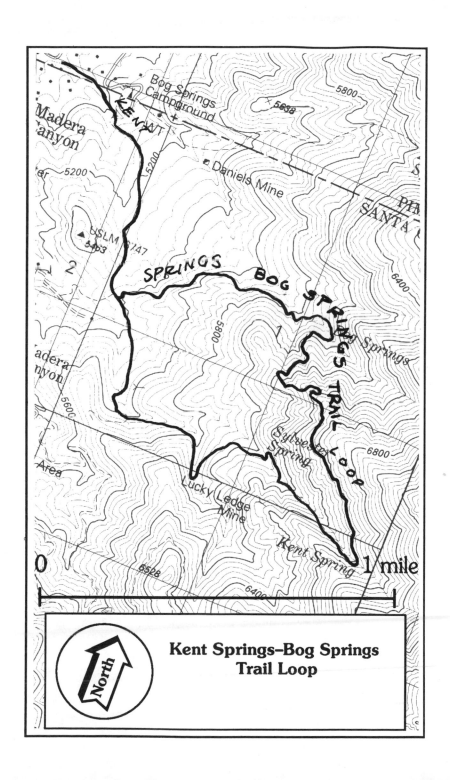

Kent Springs–Bog Springs
Trail Loop

Kent Springs–Bog Springs Trail

looking for a small sign that indicates the Bog Springs Trail. Should the sign be missing, the correct route is an obvious old jeep road that heads uphill. The route is rocky and moderately steep, gradually narrowing into a trail that goes along the right side of a deep wash. In about .2 miles the trail intersects with a wide jeep road. Turn right for .5 miles to the trailhead.

If you would rather pay the five-dollar fee, there is a large parking lot near the place where you purchase tickets to display on your car. From this parking lot, turn right and walk downhill for .1 miles. On the left is an old road and a sign indicating the beginning of the Bog Springs Trail. From this sign it is .7 miles to the actual trailhead, 1.5 miles to Bog Springs, and 2.7 miles to Kent Springs.

The route from the road into the campground begins as an old jeep road and goes down into a deep wash. (The trail from the parking area on the main road into the canyon intersects just after you climb out of this wash.) Stay on the road and avoid any side trails. The road is quite rocky and occasionally steep, going in and out of small washes. After .7 miles a sign on the left indicates the beginning of the Bog Springs Trail. Here is where you will return. You may go first to Bog Springs and then circle to Kent Springs and back to the trailhead, or reverse the direction. I prefer to hike to Bog Springs first, so the following will describe the loop in that direction.

Past the sign the trail is no longer a road, but a narrow, smooth, and sandy path. To the north and northwest, the views of Kitt Peak, the copper mines, Green Valley, and the surrounding communities stand out as you gain in elevation.

After climbing steadily for nearly a mile, the trail drops into Bog Springs. There is a concrete tank, and a spigot a short distance beyond the tank. Webster defines "bog" as "wet, spongy ground." This area comes as close to that definition as is possible in southeastern Arizona. Arizona bamboo grow in abundance. There are huge Arizona sycamore, many of them with hollowed-out trunks that would be large enough to shelter a person caught in a storm. Beyond the spring are two stone-covered tanks, again with lots of Arizona bamboo. There are huge fir trees, Arizona walnut trees and, again, many Arizona sycamore.

As the trail leaves the spring and climbs the side of the canyon, there is an almost total change in vegetation. What was a lush canyon becomes a scrub oak-covered, dry ridge. The trail switchbacks as it climbs to Kent Spring. At the point of the ridge there are excellent views of Mount Wrightson. Past this point, a few more switchbacks and you are on top of the ridge. A large log, worn smooth by many resting hikers, invites you to sit and take in the views. Now Baboquivari and Kitt peaks are visible.

Past the log, the trail is fairly level along the side of the ridge, with some moderate uphill. Several points in this area are rocky, and the shale and narrow trail make it easy to fall. As the trail goes back into the forest, it becomes easy walking again. As you approach Kent Spring, ponderosa pine begin to appear, and the area soon becomes very lush, with huge Arizona sycamores dominating the scene. There is a small stream that runs most of the year. The area is almost as lush as Bog Springs. There is a good stand of Arizona bamboo. Across the stream is a round stone tank that is Kent Spring.

At the spring, the trail goes sharply right and becomes a jeep road. It is all downhill from here on, except for a few short portions near the end. The road follows the stream down the mountain. This is a very lovely portion of the trail. After about half a mile you come to Sylvester Spring, which consists of a large concrete tank and two smaller tanks. Past the spring, the road is uphill for a very short time, and it is no longer rocky. For much of the way, the road follows the left side of the stream. At a pipeline the trail crosses the stream, and depending on the time of year, it can require wading. This entire portion along the stream is beautiful, with tall trees and the sound of running water. We saw a deer coming down to drink, and I think it would be the rare hike that you did not see some wildlife.

As the trail approaches the end, it becomes sandy, pulling away from the stream and out into the open. Depending on where you parked the car, return either the entire distance by road or cut back down the trail to the parking area in Madera Canyon.

Selected Readings

Bowden, Charles. *Frog Mountain Blues.* Tucson: The University of Arizona Press, 1987.
The Tohono O'odham Indians call the Santa Catalinas "Frog Mountain." In this essay the author warns that this unique wilderness can be lost if it becomes too available to man.

Burgess, Tony L., and Martha Ames Burgess. "Clouds, Spires and Spines." In *Tucson.* Tucson: Southwestern Mission Research Center, 1986.
An essay about the past, present, and future of the Tucson area.

Cowgill, Pete, and Eber Glendening. *Trail Guide to the Santa Catalina Mountains.* Tucson: Rainbow Expeditions, 1987.
An excellent guide to the trails of the Santa Catalina Mountains.

Gustafson, A. M., ed. *John Spring's Arizona.* Tucson: The University of Arizona Press, 1966.
A series of articles written by John Spring, a teacher and soldier in the Arizona Territory in the 1870s.

Martin, Bob, and Dotty Martin. *Hiking Guide to the Santa Rita Mountains.* Boulder, Colo.: Pruett Publishing Company, 1986.
An excellent guide to the trails of the Santa Rita Mountains.

Nabhan, Gary Paul. *Saguaro: A View of Saguaro National Monument and the Tucson Basin.* Tucson: Southwest Parks and Monuments Association, 1986.
A collection of essays about the Saguaro National Monument, with particular emphasis on the Rincon Mountain Unit.

Olin, George. *House in the Sun.* Tucson: Southwest Parks and Monuments Association, 1977.
A complete narrative about the plants and animals living in the Sonoran Desert, as well as an explanation of the desert environment.

Index

196 ○ Index

Betty Leavengood has lived in Tucson since 1969. She has taught classes at Pima Community College Community Service Division on hiking the Tucson Mountains and backpacking for ages over forty. She is currently working as a tour guide for a destination management company and leads backpacking and guided trips throughout New Mexico and Arizona.